ATLAS
OF
SHIPWRECKS
AND FORTUNES
OF THE SEA

Edited by Ian Robertson
Type set in DTLParadoxST/Helvetica Neue

ISBN: 978-0-7643-6726-7
Printed in China

Published by Schiffer Publishing, Ltd.
4880 Lower Valley Road
Atglen, PA 19310
Phone: (610) 593-1777; Fax: (610) 593-2002
Email: Info@schifferbooks.com
Web: www.schifferbooks.com

For our complete selection of fine books on this and related subjects, please visit our website at www.schifferbooks.com. You may also write for a free catalog.

Schiffer Publishing's titles are available at special discounts for bulk purchases for sales promotions or premiums. Special editions, including personalized covers, corporate imprints, and excerpts, can be created in large quantities for special needs. For more information, contact the publisher.

We are always looking for people to write books on new and related subjects. If you have an idea for a book, please contact us at proposals@schifferbooks.com.

CYRIL HOFSTEIN
Illustrations by Karin DOERING-FROGER

ATLAS
OF
SHIPWRECKS
AND FORTUNES
OF THE SEA

For Murielle and Wilfried

CONTENTS

In the expression "sea fortune," the word "fortune" has nothing to do with wealth or the search for a sunken treasure. For shipowners and insurance companies, the term first and foremost refers to a case of force majeure in the context of maritime law and is a legal fact that defines the risks inherent in seafaring, ranging from simple delays to the loss of all hands.

Just as one rigs a crossjack sail—a *voile de fortune* in French—after a storm to continue on one's journey, sailing is a game of hazard in the original sense of the word: a matter of fate, good or bad; a lucky or unlucky throw of the dice. A hesitation in a crucial moment decides whether the ship gets carried away, or whether the captain succeeds in crossing reefs that he had thought to be elsewhere.

Shipwrecks, great discoveries, mysteries, disappearances in the middle of the ocean; these tales of sea fortunes have been peddled from port to port since antiquity. Adapted, distorted, sometimes twisted: the best-known stories, such as that of the *Flying Dutchman*, are part of our maritime heritage. Many changed the course of history, such as the sinking of *La Belle*, which sounded the death knell for French North America, or the tragic loss of the English liner SS *Drummond Castle*, which led to the beaconing of the Fromveur Passage between the Molène archipelago and the island of Ushant, in the northern Iroise Sea.

Both the real and the imagined stories form part of the enigmatic legends of the oceans, this long and strange history that sailors still recount in a low voice, without being quite certain whether or not to believe it.

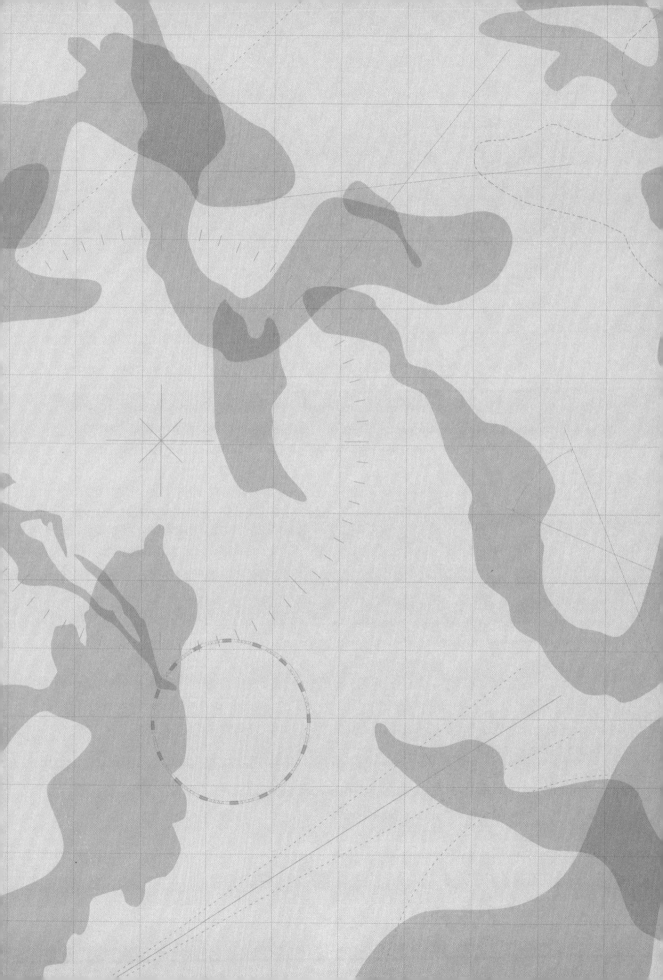

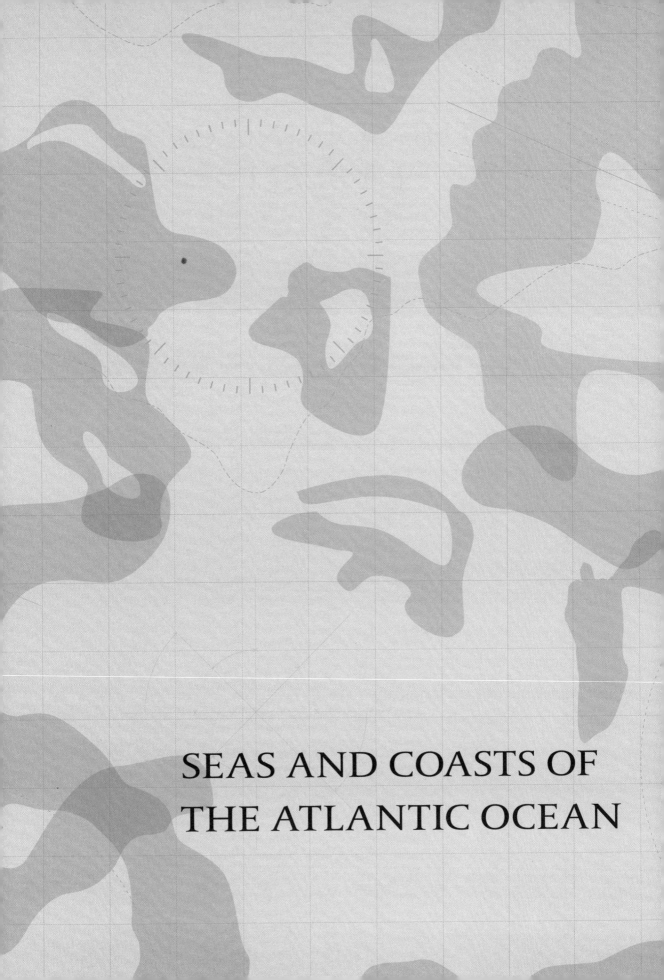

SEAS AND COASTS OF
THE ATLANTIC OCEAN

THE SINKING OF
LA BELLE

HOW FRANCE HAD ALREADY LOST AMERICA

28°34'17" N, 96°18'04" W

In the troubled waters of Matagorda Bay, on the present-day Texas coast, *La Belle* had dropped anchor—Robert Cavelier, Sieur de La Salle's last ship. His expedition to found a large French colony on the banks of the mouth of the Mississippi River and to fight the Spanish—backed by Louis XIV—turned out to be a disaster, and his men could not take it any longer. It was so hot on board that the tar of the rigging was flowing in pasty, blackish drips

> Unknowingly led astray by an imprecise map and a long course of navigation by dead reckoning, he had miscalculated by a few degrees of longitude.

across the deck. The air was heavy and oppressive, thick with a disgusting stench of sludge. Two days earlier the Indigenous Karankawa people, who kept attacking the French, had killed six sailors, including Richaud, the captain of *La Belle*. With a heavy heart, Tessier, the ship's pilot, agreed to take his place, though he would have given anything to escape this nightmare.

Since their departure from La Rochelle in July 1684, the expedition had been dogged by fate. Off Hispaniola, privateers first took the *Saint-François*, the ketch that was carrying most of the food, ammunition, and other essential goods for the fort that Cavelier was planning on establishing on the outskirts of New Mexico. Then, in Petit-Goâve, where his three other ships—*L'Aimable*, a storeship of 180 tons; *Le Joly*, a two-deck man-of-war with thirty-four guns; and *La Belle*, specially built at Rochefort—were stopping over, most of the passengers (about three hundred men, women, and children) fell ill. The discipline on board took a hit, some soldiers deserted, and the settlers, overwhelmed by the heat and tropical fever, refused to leave the island. The relationship between the naval officers and the viceroy of Louisiana—an enormous province that extended up to the Great Lakes, which the viceroy had claimed "in the name of His Majesty Louis the Fourteenth" in 1682—could not have been worse. After two months of waiting, the three ships finally weighed their anchors

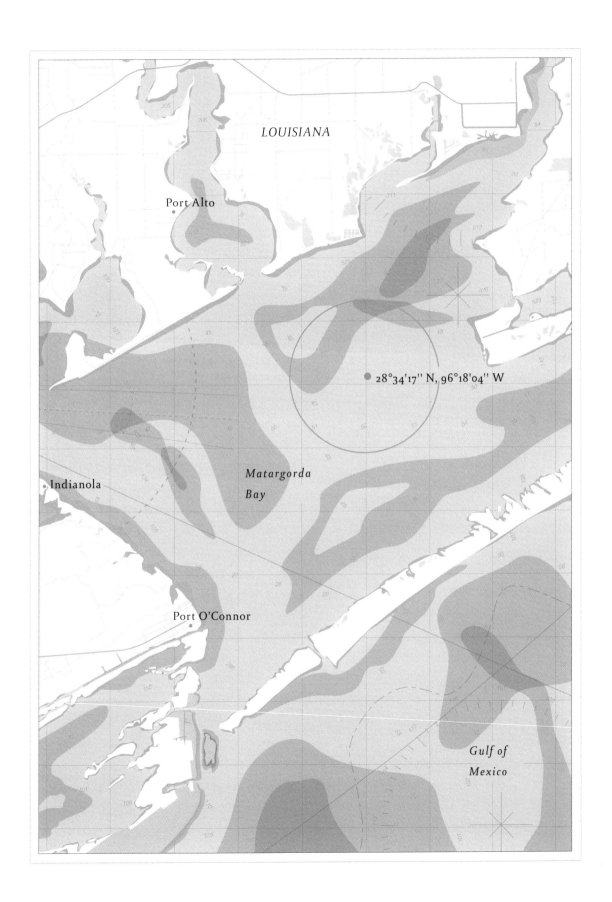

LOUISIANA

Port Alto

28°34'17'' N, 96°18'04'' W

Matargorda
Bay

Indianola

Port O'Connor

Gulf of
Mexico

and sailed into the Gulf of Mexico on December 12.

Two weeks later, land was in sight. What a relief. But Cavelier de La Salle did not recognize the coastline. Nothing reminded him of the familiar landscape. Unknowingly led astray by an imprecise map and a

> The fanatic adventurer, who had managed to gain the confidence of Versailles by piquing the court's interest with his stories of vast spaces, had become a mere shadow of his former self.

long course of navigation by dead reckoning, he had miscalculated by a few degrees of longitude.

On February 4, 1685, after three days of fog, the fleet finally reached what looked like an arm of the Mississippi River, which he christened Colbert River. But during the maneuver, *L'Aimable* ran aground in shallow

waters. Despite the crew's efforts to plug the leak, the ship sank with all its load, and four cannons were lost. Cavelier and Beaujeu, the captain of *Le Joly*, were quick to accuse each other of incompetence. The debate got heated and the vessel ended up sailing for France, taking with it other discouraged or disgraced emigrants. The officer offered one last time to return if Cavelier encountered the mouth of the Mississippi. But in a hurry to move on, La Salle refused. Ironically, Beaujeu would hit upon it 435 miles (700 kilometers) farther east, just days after leaving, and drew up a new map. Left to their own devices, the remaining two hundred settlers struggled to survive. In this apocalyptic atmosphere, men, women, and children took turns to clear land, erect enclosures, and establish a garrison they called Fort Saint Louis. Later, La Salle, still eager to find the river, left the colony, coming and going at will to pursue his vain attempts, returning each time more embittered than before. The fanatic adventurer, who had managed to gain the confidence of Versailles by piquing the court's interest with his stories of vast spaces and huge territories that could be grabbed off the Spanish Crown, had become a mere shadow of his former self.

At the helm of *La Belle*, Captain Tessier eventually got bored and spent most of his time emptying the wine reserve. The sea was pewter gray, dreary, and thick.

One evening, while some sailors set out to procure water with the only raft on board, he opted to hang a small candle on the yard, instead of a lantern, which was quickly extinguished by the wind. None of them would return. Exhausted, the survivors staged a mutiny. But they were unable to steer the ship alone and ended up begging Tessier to take them ashore. As often happened in this bay, the wind turned northerly and the swell increased. Drunker than ever, the captain lost control of the ship, and it was tossed around by the ever-growing waves. The crew tried to drop anchor, but the ship began to list and filled with water. Only six men reached the shore. At Fort Saint Louis a handful of French people still guarded the remains of the colony. But the savage murder of La Salle by his own men on March 17, 1687, during a final strained attempt to capture the Mississippi River, left them permanently defenseless. On Christmas Eve 1688, the Karankawa people ambushed the village and spared only four children. Guarded by tribeswomen, they were later exchanged for axes and tools from Spanish scouts. What remains of Robert Cavelier de La Salle's great American dream are only some ruins, a handful of dismantled cannons, and the wreck of *La Belle*, which was discovered in 1995, three centuries after it sank, almost intact. Archeologists from the Texas Historical Commission are still trying to interpret what they found at the bottom of the sea at Matagorda Bay.

What remains of Robert Cavelier de La Salle's great American dream are only some ruins, a handful of dismantled cannons, and the wreck of La Belle.

IN SEARCH OF L'OISEAU BLANC

WHAT HAPPENED TO NUNGESSER AND COLI?

46°39'30" N, 53°04'25" W

Even though multiple experts have raised heaven and earth over the years to try to solve the enigma of the disappearance of Nungesser and Coli's plane L'Oiseau Blanc, not a single trace has been found of their biplane, a Levasseur PL.8, which they used in their attempt to fly across the North Atlantic from France to New York. Neither its engine nor its wings nor any other debris remains. Nothing but the ocean as far as the eye can see.

On May 8, 1927, at dawn, when the two heroes departed from Bourget, the whole of France held its breath. Their diligently prepared challenge made the headlines of every newspaper. Charles Nungesser was a legend of the Great War, a flamboyant ace with forty-three air combat victories to his name and a seductive daredevil. More reserved perhaps, François Coli, his navigator, was no less experienced. Seriously injured in 1918, the merchant navy officer managed the double crossing of the Mediterranean the following year and broke the distance record for a straight-line flight between Paris and Kénitra, Morocco. Level headed and precise, he was the ideal travel companion. To make their plane lighter, the aviators decided not to take a radio, calculating that for a flight of thirty-two to thirty-five hours at 100 mph (160 km/h), this would reduce their necessary fuel reserves to 836 gallons (3,800 liters). A few minutes after takeoff they were spotted above Étretat, France, near Cowes in England, and in Ireland before heading for New York, where tens of thousands of people awaited them. In Paris, the Aéro-Club de France already celebrated their triumphal arrival at the Statue of Liberty, and several newspapers published special issues. But L'Oiseau Blanc disappeared.

> In Paris, the Aéro-Club de France already celebrated their triumphal arrival at the Statue of Liberty. But L'Oiseau Blanc disappeared.

On the morning of May 10, the rescue team crisscrossed the Channel from the

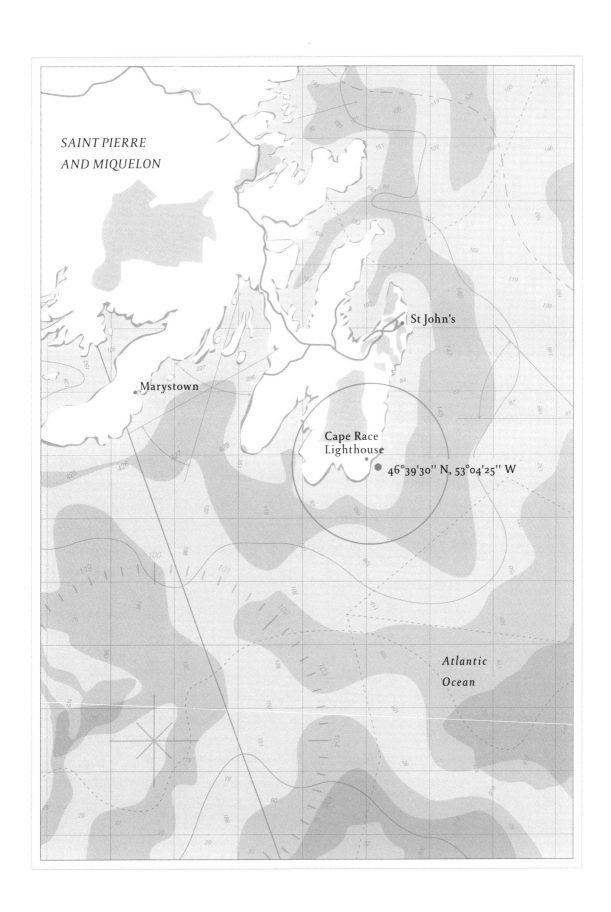

SAINT PIERRE
AND MIQUELON

St John's

Marystown

Cape Race
Lighthouse
46°39'30" N, 53°04'25" W

Atlantic
Ocean

A tragic misunderstanding, in the toxic context of Prohibition, might have allowed the American Charles Lindbergh to become a legend twelve days after their departure, when he became the first pilot to fly solo from New York to Paris at the helm of the famous Spirit of Saint Louis.

French Côte d'Albâtre to England, though there was no sight of a wreckage.

On the other side of the Atlantic, Canadian and American vessels searched the Gulf of St. Lawrence, Newfoundland, and the sea around Sable Island and Nova Scotia because, on May 9, a dozen witnesses reportedly saw or heard a plane passing at low altitude. Among them was Pierre-Marie Le Chevalier, a fisherman from Saint-Pierre, who recounted having heard the sound of an engine brutally coming to a halt. That morning, near Cap Noir, hidden in the mist, his dog had also barked at the top of his lungs. There were no other clues. The search was finally abandoned on June 9, and only Australian aviator Sidney Cotton continued to comb the area in his seaplane, without success.

The official line is that L'Oiseau Blanc must have been caught in a squall or come off course in the fog, then crashed somewhere in the ocean. But in the 1980s, new findings suggested that the aircraft could have crashed in a very isolated region of Maine, so Roland Nungesser, the aviator's nephew, decided to reopen the case. In vain. For a second time, the lead did not come to anything. If Bernard Decré, who devoted several expeditions to the search for the two pilots, is to be believed, this is what might have happened: in sight of the American coast, L'Oiseau Blanc first skirted along the east coast of Newfoundland, guided by the breakers, before heading due south to the Cape Race lighthouse. At least three boats traveling the same route spotted it: The *Albert*, a Danish three-master; the *Armistice*, a schooner departing from Granville, France; and the *Modoc*, a US Coast Guard patrol boat tasked with intercepting alcohol traffickers who were constantly tacking along the border between the United States, Canada, and Saint Pierre and Miquelon. After thirty-three hours in the air and without any other means of communication, Decré speculates, Nungesser and Coli wanted to report their location and announce their imminent arrival in Manhattan by navigating toward the ships under their flight path. A friendly but fatal turn. Because Decré is certain: the American Coast Guard mistook the plane for a bootlegger aircraft, or smugglers confused it with one of the police's biplanes, and L'Oiseau Blanc was shot down. A tragic misunderstanding, in the toxic context of Prohibition, might have allowed American Charles Lindbergh to become a legend twelve days after their departure, when he became the first pilot to fly solo from New York to Paris—between May 20 and 21, 1927—at the helm of the famous Spirit of Saint Louis. One might think it was a conspiracy . . .

THE FICTITIOUS SHIPWRECK OF THE COMTE DE BOISJOURDAIN

THE INCREDIBLE STORY BEHIND THE CHASLES COLLECTION

SOMEWHERE IN THE ATLANTIC

In 1791, fleeing the French Revolution, the Comte de Boisjourdain—one of the greatest bibliophiles of his time—died a hero when the ship that was taking him to America sank. The story of the disaster is blood-curdling. In the wreck, which crashed but was still afloat, there was chaos and desolation galore. Women in tears pleaded for their children to be saved. Sailors, raptured by madness, hurled themselves into the waves. In an attempt to help them, the Comte de Boisjourdain drowned, while what re-

> In an attempt to help them, the Comte de Boisjourdain drowned, while what remained of the ship was tossed by the swell and disappeared in the depths.

mained of the ship was tossed by the swell and disappeared in the depths. Miraculously spared, part of his library was saved and returned to his family before falling into oblivion. In 1860 his last descendant, crippled by debt, was ready to part with it. But he wanted this transaction to be conducted with the utmost discretion—noblesse oblige. Knowing the famous mathematician Michel Chasles's passion for historic artifacts, Denis Vrain-Lucas, a paleographer who worked in the genealogical office Courtois-Letellier, suggested to the penniless gentleman that he act as his intermediary. And so, in 1861, a mesmerized Chasles discovered the extent of the collection amassed by the Comte de Boisjourdain. Among the documents that Vrain-Lucas presented to him (and that had passed through his hands) were letters by Molière, Racine, and Pythagoras; from Alexander the Great to Aristotle; from the resurrected Lazarus to Saint Peter; and from Cleopatra to Julius Caesar. There was also a pass for safe passage granted by Vercingetorix to Pompey, and missives signed by the very hands of Judas Iscariot, Pontius Pilate, Joan of Arc, Rabelais, Charles V, Shakespeare, Galileo, Montesquieu, Cicero, and even Dante Alighieri . . . this was undoubtedly too good to be true.

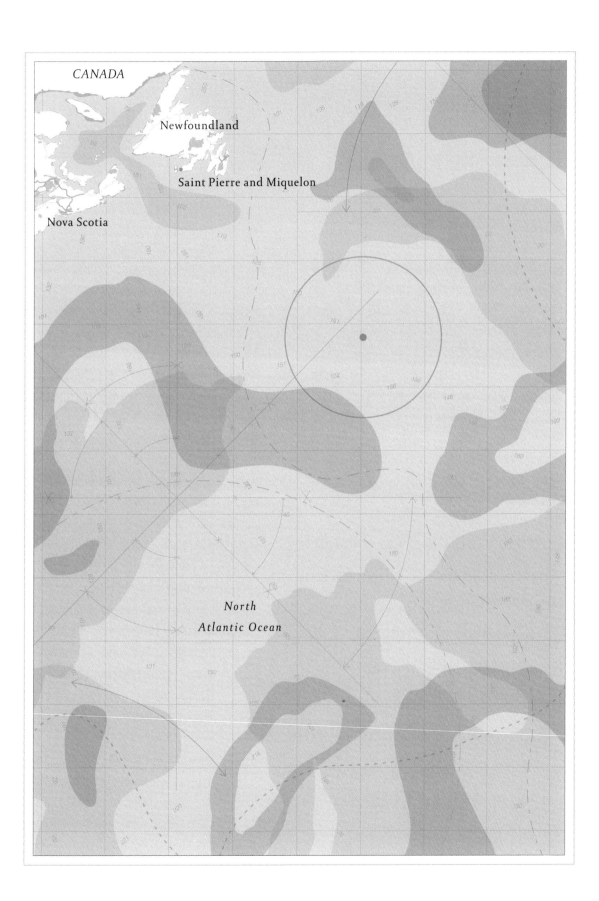

CANADA

Newfoundland

Saint Pierre and Miquelon

Nova Scotia

North
Atlantic Ocean

But the scientist absolutely wanted to believe they were genuine, and bought the whole lot, spending nearly 140,000 gold francs—a fortune!—over several years on blatantly forged documents written in a fantastical old French on artificially aged paper. Because Vrain-Lucas had made the whole thing up: the shipwreck in 1791, the Comte de Boisjourdain, and even his heir! This autodidact—the son of a day laborer and a maid—who had worked at times as a law clerk, at the Châteaudun court, and then at the mortgage registry, was a talented forger, and Michel Chasles was his golden goose. The ecstatic mathematician kept asking him for further documents, which he would accumulate, sometimes without even looking at them. Vrain-Lucas carried out the orders and even presented him, with a straight face, a threatening letter from Cain to Abel. But the well-oiled machine eventually got stuck. On July 8, 1867, at the French Académie des Sciences, in front of a group of eminent scientists, Chasles solemnly declared that the laws of gravitation had not been discovered by Newton, but by Blaise Pascal. And that he had irrefutable proof: two letters addressed to Isaac Newton in which the French philosopher explained this mathematical principle. The audience held its breath. But the letters invented by Vrain-Lucas were dated to a time when Newton would have been a mere twelve years old. . . . A clash of experts ensued and, after polemics lasting two years, the crook who

> Because Vrain-Lucas had made the whole thing up: the shipwreck in 1791, the Comte de Boisjourdain, and even his heir! This autodidact—the son of a day laborer and a maid—who had worked at times as a law clerk, at the Châteaudun court, and then at the mortgage registry, was a talented forger, and Michel Chasles was his golden goose.

had forged more than 27,000 signatures, letters, documents, and manuscripts, one as fake as the next, was unmasked and arrested on September 9, 1869.

Among general amusement, Chasles, who admitted to having been fooled, became the butt of ridicule. Sentenced to two years in prison, a fine of 500 francs, and the cost of the court proceedings, Vrain-Lucas was paying for his fraud. Yet, he would succumb to his penchant for forgery twice more and be sent behind bars before dying in his bed in 1880 at age eighty-eight.

THE *FLYING DUTCHMAN*

THE MYSTERY OF THE GHOST SHIP

34°21'30" S, 18°28'15" E

A book about sea fortunes would be incomplete without a chapter on the *Flying Dutchman*. Stories about ghost ships have always had their firm place in sailors' lore, and this one, peddled from port to port over generations, is a delicate tidbit.

> A spirit or a ghost is then said to have appeared to him, pronouncing an eternal curse. Since then, perpetually caught in stormy weather, the ship has been condemned to aimlessly sail the seas between Cape Horn and the Cape of Good Hope …

The story always begins more or less the same way. Pressed to pass the Cape of Good Hope and deliver his cargo as quickly as possible, a Dutch captain refused to let his exhausted crew rest. A storm was raging overhead, but the captain was having none of it and even shot one of the sailors who implored him to be reasonable. He was the sole master on board after God, and, his chest swelled with pride and roaring with laughter, he was not afraid to scream this terrible dare into the wind: "I will round this cape, even if I must sail until the end of time!" A spirit or a ghost is then said to have appeared to him, pronouncing an eternal curse. Since then, perpetually caught in stormy weather, the ship has been condemned to aimlessly sail the seas between Cape Horn and the Cape of Good Hope . . .

In 1834, German poet Heinrich Heine tackled the subject matter and added a detail that would change everything. He allowed the captain one day ashore once every seven years, and the caveat that he would be delivered from his curse if he met a woman willing to love him and accompany him to his death. Then, 117 years later, Hollywood took Heine's version literally and offered the role of the *Flying Dutchman* to James Mason, and that of his lover to the sublime Ava Gardner. In between, in 1839, English writer Frederick

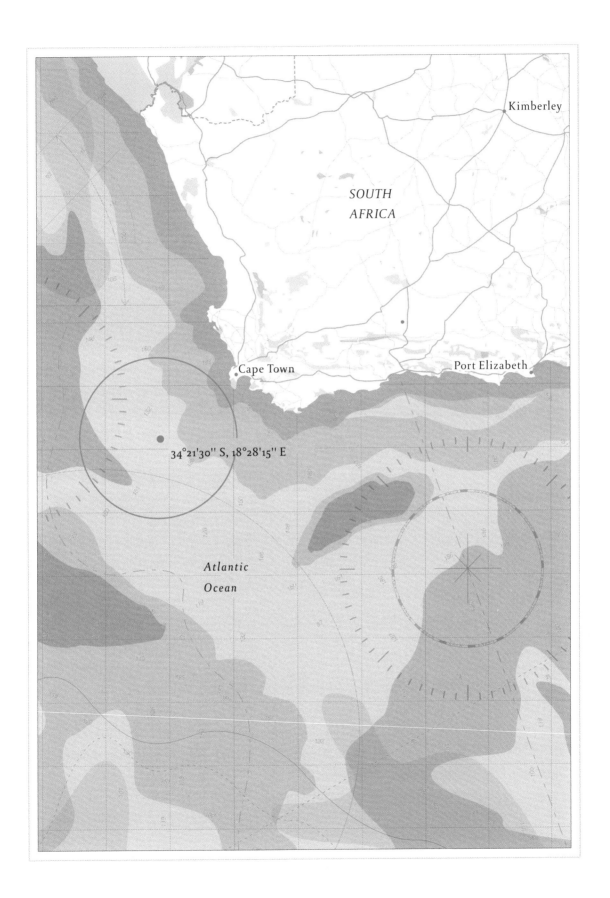

Kimberley

SOUTH
AFRICA

Cape Town

Port Elizabeth

34°21'30" S, 18°28'15" E

Atlantic
Ocean

Marryat published *The Phantom Ship*, a novel whose protagonist, Philip Vanderdecken, the son of the cursed captain, has a curious encounter as his ship approaches the Cape of Good Hope:

"In the centre of the pale light, which extended about fifteen degrees above the horizon, there was indeed a large ship about three miles distant; but, although it was a perfect calm, she was to all appearance buffeting in a violent gale, plunging and lifting over a surface that was smooth as glass, now careening to her bearing, then recovering herself. . . . Each minute

Yet, in 1835, a British captain said he saw a large ship race toward him before mysteriously disappearing ...

she was plainer to the view. At last, she was seen to wear, and in so doing, before she was brought to the wind on the other tack, she was so close to them that they could distinguish the men on board . . . ;

and then the gloom gradually rose, and in a few seconds she had totally disappeared." Everyone now knows the legend. Richard Wagner, who feared for his life on a rough sea journey to England, turned the captain into a romantic opera hero seeking redemption, and Victor Hugo, in *The Legend of the Ages*, dedicated some of his most beautiful verses to him:

It is the Dutchman, the barque
Branded with the flaming finger's mark!
The cursed man-of-war!
Hoisted his villainous sail!
The sinister pirate with evil hail
Is sailing forevermore.

But did he really exist? According to several naval historians, Bernard Fokke, a captain at the service of the Dutch East India Company at the end of the seventeenth century, could have served as a model. This extraordinary navigator, famous in his day, was indeed known for making the trip from Amsterdam to Java in just three months and four days; that is, about two months faster than usual. A real feat. The disbelief of his contemporaries, in addition to his extreme ugliness, might have caused envious rivals to accuse him of signing a pact with the devil and flying across the seven seas.

At some point, imagination took the relay from reality. No more, no less. No madness, no curse, and thus no ghost.

Yet, in 1835, a British captain said he saw a large ship race toward him before mysteriously disappearing . . . on July 11, 1881, along the Australian coast aboard the training ship *La Bacchante* en route to Sydney, the future king of England, George V, witnessed the strange appearance of a large sailboat that passed in silence and suddenly vanished. In March 1939, not far from a beach in South Africa, a vessel suddenly emerged, spinning on the waves, all sails hoisted, although there was no wind, before disappearing into the water. And during the Battle of the Atlantic, a German U-boat crew was said to have seen the *Flying Dutchman* . . . but no one has since come across him. Has the Dutchman finally found his soulmate?

Stories about ghost ships have always had their firm place in sailors' lore, and this one, peddled from port to port over generations, is a delicate tidbit.

THE DRAMA OF
LA MIGNONETTE

HOW THREE SAILORS SURVIVED BY EATING THE FOURTH

25°43'28" S, 08°27'13" W

In Edgar Alan Poe's peculiar novel published in 1838, *The Narrative of Arthur Gordon Pym of Nantucket*, there is a scene that lets cold shivers run down the reader's spine. Eaten up by hunger, Richard Parker, one of the sailors trapped in the floating wreck of the brig the *Grampus*, on which the protagonist had embarked as a

> Eaten up by hunger, Richard Parker, one of the sailors trapped in the floating wreck of the brig the Grampus, on which the protagonist had embarked as a stowaway, proposes to his fellow sufferers to draw straws to determine one of the four survivors to be sacrificed to save the other three.

stowaway, proposes to his fellow sufferers to draw straws to determine one of the four survivors to be sacrificed to save the other three. Horrified by this proposal, Pym firmly refuses, ready to "suffer death

in any shape or under any circumstances rather than resort to such a course." Within the confined space of the unmasted ship, the men size each other up and closely watch one another, a knife always at hand. After resisting this terrible act with all his might, Pym eventually gives in. Ironically, Parker is the one to draw the short straw. "I must not dwell upon the fearful repast which immediately ensued," says the frightened young man. "Such things may be imagined, but words have no power to impress the mind with the exquisite horror of their reality." But fifty years later, reality caught up with fiction, when three survivors from the shipwrecked English yacht the *Mignonette* were brought to justice before the highest court of the United Kingdom for having devoured the fourth: a seventeen-year-old cabin boy by the name of . . . Richard Parker.

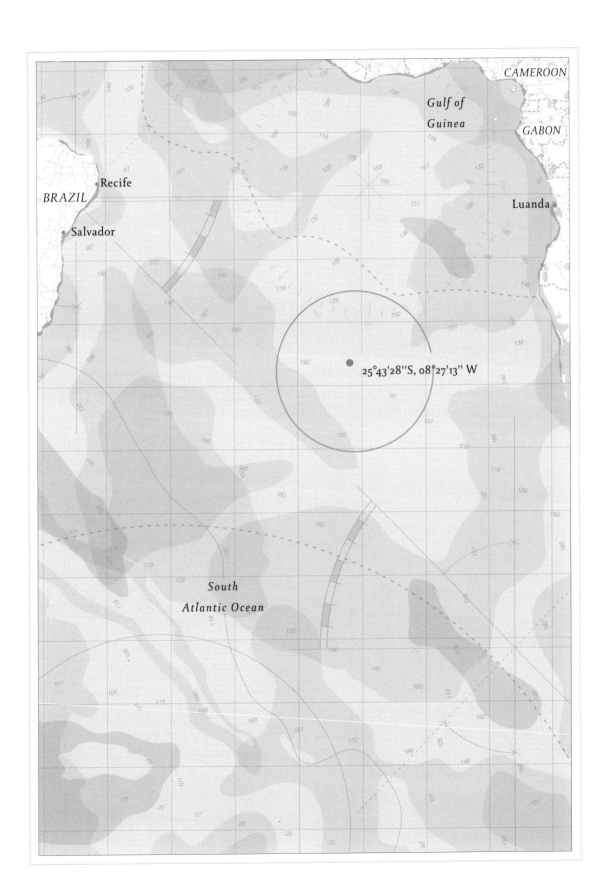

25°43'28''S, 08°27'13'' W

Departing Southampton for the Australian coast on May 19, 1884, the *Mignonette* is heading for the South Atlantic and is about 1,600 nautical miles from the Cape of Good Hope when a huge wave hits it head on. The 52-foot boat (16 meters) immediately capsizes and threatens to sink. In a panic, Captain Tom Dudley makes his three crew get into the lifeboat, tak-

Faced with the magistrates and an eager British public, the cannibals tell their terrible story with a mixture of candor and naivety.

ing with him his navigational instruments and two large cans of turnips, but no water. For the first three days the crew tries to ignore their hunger and thirst. On the fourth, on July 7, they cannot hold on any longer and open one of the cans, whose notorious taste of metal and

rancidness seems to them as sweet as honey. The next day the catch of a turtle makes for a change, and thanks to the last ration of turnips, the men endure a little longer. Then for eight days nothing happens. No food or water and no ship in sight. Nothing. Against everyone's advice, Parker drinks seawater and quickly falls ill. Stretched out in the bilge of the boat, he begins to hallucinate and, caught by convulsions, falls into a coma. Each passing hour is torture, and on July 16 or 17 the captain finally suggests drawing lots to determine who might be eaten by the others. But Edmond Brooks, one of the sailors, refuses. The following day, Dudley brings up the matter again and this time suggests killing the least capable of the four. By default the young Parker, whose condition continues to worsen, is condemned to death. More than just a fixed idea, eating him has become the obvious choice. Brooks is still reluctant, but Edwin Stephens, the fourth in the group, agrees straightaway. By two votes to one, the cabin boy's fate is sealed on July 25.

On July 29, just four days after the crime, the German three-mast barque *Montezu-*

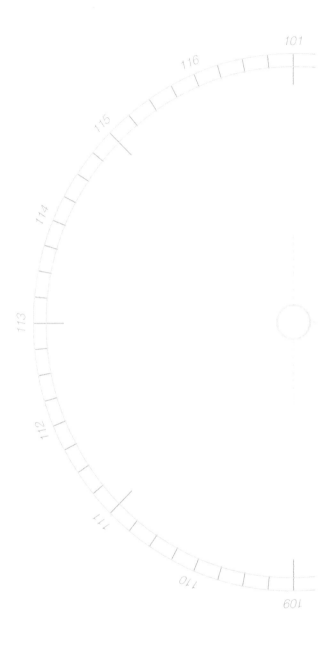

ma picks up the three shipwrecked sailors and takes them to Falmouth, England, where Dudley and Stephens are charged with culpable homicide and Brooks with cannibalism. Faced with the magistrates and an eager British public, the cannibals tell their terrible story with a mixture of candor and naivety that make even the most-hardened souls melt. To the extent that no one knows what to judge anymore: a sordid murder or the animalistic instinct to stay alive at all cost? The first two, who did not contest the facts and swore to have acted out of necessity, are sentenced to death, and the third is released. But on the advice of her home secretary Sir William Harcourt, Queen Victoria exercises her prerogative of mercy, and their sentence is commuted on December 12 to six months of imprisonment. The public, which eventually picked the side of the three sailors and their troubling hideous crime, is satisfied. But their case, still studied by law students today, weighs heavily on the conscience of the British justice system.

THE SHIP GRAVEYARD OF LANDÉVENNEC

WHERE GRAND DREAMS COME TO DIE

48°17'16" N, 04°16'38" W

After serving as a breakwater in front of the naval school and rusting away in the ship graveyard of Landévennec, the *Aconit* eventually returned to sea to be brought to a dismantling site in Belgium. A few years earlier, the frigate would have probably been sunk offshore, but this practice has been banned in Europe, and warships

Alongside the *Aconit*, dozens of other ships have dropped anchor at Landévennec, where they are calmly awaiting the guillotine. The cove of Penforn has long been home to the reserve squadron of the port of Brest.

destined for the scrap heap are now rotting away at the berth. Built at the end of the 1960s and put into active service in 1973, this legacy vessel of the Free French Naval Forces, although famous for destroying two German submarines in one day in 1943, is one of the few units of the French navy that have never really lived up to their promise. First used as a corvette and destined to inaugurate a new series specialized in antisubmarine warfare, the *Aconit* had to go on a self-finding mission. Turned into a frigate, she changed her hull number twice and tried to deliver what was expected of her. But on February 27, 1997, the final word was spoken. Retired prematurely as part of a plan to shrink the French fleet, she was decommissioned and her name was transferred to the fourth stealth frigate of the La Fayette class, already waiting in line.

Alongside the *Aconit*, dozens of other ships have dropped anchor at Landévennec, where they are calmly awaiting the guillotine. Nestled at the south end of the natural harbor of Brest, on the last meander of the Aulne River that wraps around the island of Térénez, the cove of Penforn has long been home to the reserve squadron of the port of Brest. But the French navy eventually turned it into a kind of anchorage waiting room, and then

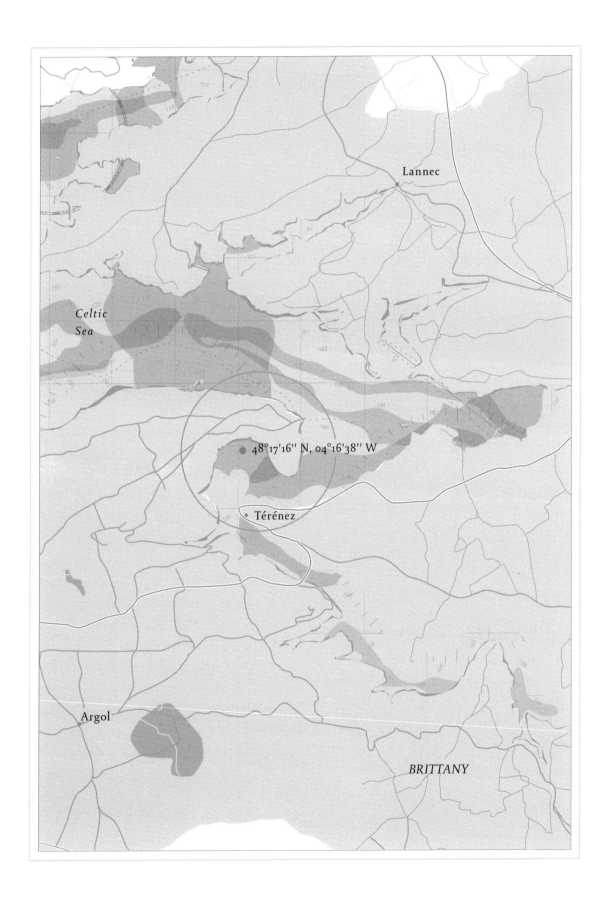

into a graveyard for the ships no longer fit for service. Moored fore and aft between two other hulls eaten away by salt and spray, the ex-cruiser *Colbert*, who took French general Charles de Gaulle on an official visit to Canada in 1967, remained there until 2016.

> Browsing the long list of decommissioned ships, you rediscover the glory of bygone times, with the frigate *De Grasse*, the aviso-escort *Enseigne de Vaisseau Henry*, or the escort for the antisubmarine squadron, *La Galissonnière*.

After more than ten years at the mooring, the *Ernest Brown*, a tug built for the Normandy landings on June 6, 1944, sadly was broken up. Like her, the unusual *Kometa*, a Soviet-designed hydrofoil from the 1970s that sailed from Le Conquet to Ushant in twenty minutes (at 34 knots) under the flag of Vedettes Armoricaines, ended her journey here alongside the old transrades *L'Ondine*, *Faune*, and *Néréide* and the P400-class patrol vessels *La Boudeuse*, *La Fougueuse*, and *La Railleuse*. Browsing the long list of decommissioned ships, you rediscover the glory of bygone times, with the frigate *De Grasse*, the aviso-escort *Enseigne de Vaisseau Henry*, or the escort for the antisubmarine squadron, *La Galissonnière*. Thanks to the battleship *Flandre*, the transport and hospital sailboat *Armorique*, the minesweeper *Alençon*, and the liberty ships *Le Verdon*, *Courseulles*, and *Orléans*, you can explore the regions and cities of France. You also have the opportunity to flick through the herbarium of French navy minesweepers: the *Capucine*, *Dahlia*, *Hortensia*, *OEillet*, *Pétunia*, and *Tulipe* all were demolished one after the other in the 1980s. The former aircraft carrier *Clemenceau* was to join them, but the narrow passage of the Capelan sandbank and its shallow waters made its transfer impossi-

THE *THÉSEE*

A SAD DAY FOR MONSIEUR DE CONFLANS

47°19'56" N, 02°45'59" W

The French navy's minesweeper *Cassiopée* slowly traveled southwest of the Vilaine estuary, about 11 nautical miles from Le Croisic and 6 miles from Hoëdic Island. Then the vessel let two divers in the water. In the muddy and murky sea, they perceived a large amount of wood under the sediment. The team of enthusiasts was holding their collective breath: they had

> The team of enthusiasts was holding their collective breath: they had spent years conducting searches to find the *Thésée*, a French "seventy-four" sunk during the Battle of Quiberon Bay, a terrible defeat at sea in the middle of a storm on November 20, 1759.

spent years conducting searches to find the *Thésée*, a French "seventy-four" sunk during the Battle of Quiberon Bay, a terrible defeat at sea in the middle of a storm on November 20, 1759. Two months later, the *André Malraux*, one of the ships of the French Department of Underwater Archaeological Research (DRASSM), arrived to check the area. At a depth of 66 feet (20 meters) under the sea, the archeologists confirmed the discovery of the wreckage of the ship lost during its first battle in Quiberon Bay.

On that day, three years after the start of the Seven Years' War, France, which dreamed of landing its troops in Scotland to challenge the king of Great Britain on land, lost six of its most important ships. Sure of himself, however, Admiral de Conflans, who was heading toward Belle-Île, had decided to return to the bay in the hope of finding refuge. But English admiral Edward Hawke immediately attacked de Conflans's rearguard. The *Formidable*, an eighty-gun ship, fought back fiercely and avoided being sunk. Among the survivors was the young Lapérouse, the future Pacific explorer. The *Héros* was subsequently forced to admit defeat.

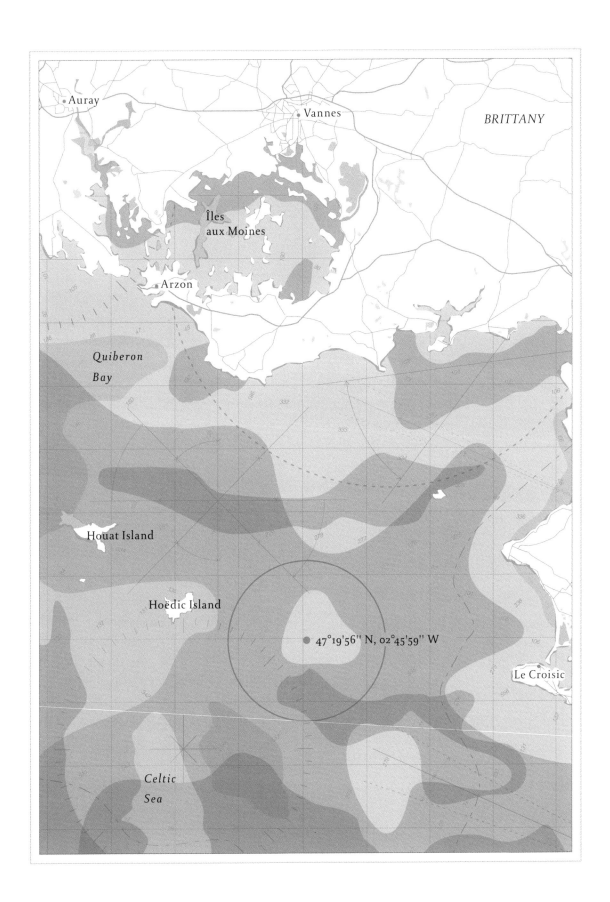

The wind had picked up and was constantly changing direction, making it impossible to form a line of battle. With its twenty-three ships the English squadron gave the French no chance. During a support maneuver, two seventy-fours, the *Superbe* and the *Thésée*, disappeared in the increasingly powerful waves. Forced to hastily turn into the swell, the hatches of her lower battery remained open,

Forced to hastily turn into the swell, the hatches of her lower battery remained open, and the *Thésée* sank without firing a single gunshot, taking with her 630 men. Only twenty-two sailors, clinging to the masts that still protruded from the waves, were rescued.

and the *Thésée* sank without firing a single gunshot, taking with her 630 men, among them Guy-François Kersaint, Comte de Coëtnempren, her captain, and two of his sons, Jacques Guy-François and Guy-François. Only twenty-two sailors, clinging to the masts that still protruded from the waves, were rescued. On the evening of the battle, the *Soleil Royal*, the flagship with its eighty guns, ran aground just off Le Croisic, followed by the *Héros*. The *Juste*, a seventy-gun ship, got into distress and sank at the mouth of the Loire.

The English lost only two ships: the *Essex* and the *Resolution*, slashed open on the shallow reefs of the Plateau du Four. To prevent her from being captured, Conflans gave orders to set the *Soleil Royal* alight. Making the most of the inferno, several English vessels approached and set fire to the *Héros*. Eight ships of the fleet led by the vice admiral of the Flotte du Ponant fled to Rochefort, and eleven more were trapped in the Vilaine estuary, kettled by a British blockade. It was a disaster. Conflans landed with the crew of the *Soleil Royal* and handed his sword back to the commander of Le Croisic with these prophetic words:

"Here, sir; I doubt I will have use for it again." The defeat was too great. His officers blamed him, Versailles no longer wanted anything to do with him, and a pamphlet published in Nantes harshly mocked his sailors: "Thersites's descendants, heroic and bold, took the signal to fight for a signal to bolt!" Did they even know what they were fighting for? The conflict pitching the kingdom of France, together with Austria and Russia and their allies, against the British Empire and Prussia was so toxic that central Europe and its colonies in the Americas and Asia were being put to fire and the sword. Nothing seems to stop the belligerent parties. Carried away by their game of alliances, they competed tirelessly on land and sea. In this warfaring world, the Battle of Quiberon Bay was only a sidenote, but the French Royal Navy paid dearly and definitively lost its rank at sea. The oceans were now flying the Union Jack.

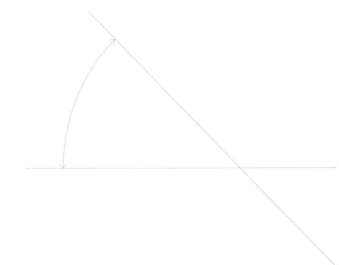

THE BONAPARTES' BARGE BEHIND CLOSED DOORS

A DINGHY WORTHY OF EMPERORS

———

48°23'25'' N, 04°29'12'' E

Assembled in just twenty-one days so that the emperor could inspect the new arsenal at Antwerp in a dignified way, Napoleon I's barge will have spent very little time at sea. Built by master shipbuilder Théau, originally from Granville, France, following plans by engineer Guillemard and decorated by sculptor Van Petersen, she measures almost 60 feet (more than 18 meters) in length and 10 feet (3.3 meters) in width and features a curious, delicately gilded deckhouse that would have been more appropriate for a carriage than a rowboat. But the aim was first and foremost to please the victor of Austerlitz, who liked neither the sea nor sailors. On April 30, 1810, the heavily adorned craft entered Antwerp heralded by applause. Napoleon and young Empress Marie-Louise were on board, accompanied by Marshal Berthier, the minister of the navy, Denis Decrès, and Admiral Missiessy, commander of the Escaut Squadron. Twenty-eight National Guard sailors ensured the safe passage of the imperial couple who visited the flagship, the *Charlemagne*, attended the launch of the eighty-gun ship *Friedland* and inspected the entire fleet. Afterward the barge was laid up in dock for months. After Bonaparte's abdication and the fall of Antwerp in 1814, Louis XVIII had her sent to Brest, where she gradually fell into oblivion. In August 1858, the barge was refurbished to allow

Emperor Napoleon III and Empress Eugénie to visit the harbor and port before traveling up the Penfeld River to Villeneuve. Entirely decorated according to the taste of the Second Empire, she features a striking figurehead representing Neptune holding his trident, flanked by cherubim and dolphins. At the stern, just above the deckhouse, four cherubs support a huge golden imperial crown made of wood.

During the Third Republic, Félix Faure, in 1896, and Émile Loubet, in 1902, used her now and then without dismantling the extravagant décor of the fallen emperor. Republican pomp did not despise the gilding of bygone days. On November 19, 1922, the great barge set for the sea one last time during a ceremony in celebration of the triumph of the French Naval School. Stored at the back of the arsenal, the barge returned to Paris in May 1943 to escape the Allied bombardments that pounded the submarine base of the first and ninth U-boat flotillas. But on arrival, the gates of the Musée national de la Marine turned out to be too narrow. In August 1945, after much pondering, a huge hole was punched into the walls of the Palais de Chaillot, where the emperor's barge had been enclosed for seventy-three years. In October 2018 the ship that saw so many visitors march past it left Paris for good and returned to Brest, her historical home port.

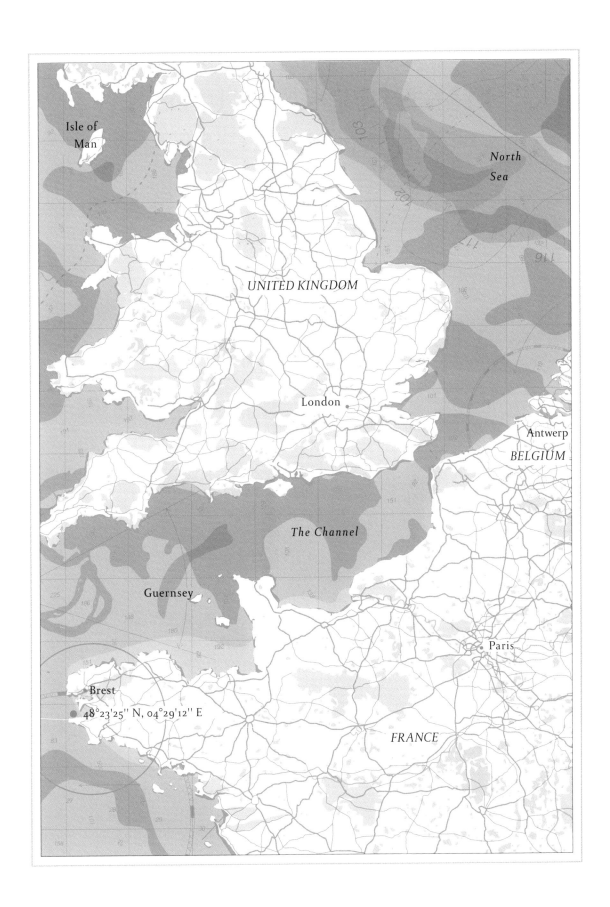

Isle of
Man

North
Sea

UNITED KINGDOM

London

Antwerp

BELGIUM

The Channel

Guernsey

Paris

Brest
48°23'25'' N, 04°29'12'' E

FRANCE

THE SIREN OF THE SS *DRUMMOND CASTLE*

A MEMORY KEPT BY THE ISLANDS

48°23'03'' N, 05°02'33'' W

In Molène and Ushant, no one will ever forget the tragedy of the SS *Drummond Castle*, the great British liner shattered on the Pierre-Vertes reef at the entrance to the Fromveur Passage. It remains unclear why she was there, on the night of June 16, 1896, in the heart of this very dangerous passage with tidal currents that

> The lifeboats were ready to be launched. But in less than ten minutes, the liner sank straight down, without having had time to set off a mayday call or rescue the passengers.

are among the strongest in the world. Some say that Captain William Pierce had miscalculated and believed the ship to be in safe waters, convinced that he had passed the Ponant Isles. Others blame the thick fog that veiled the tip of Brittany, and infer that the party that took place on deck the night before the arrival back in London might have made a few heads spin with lethal consequences. Immediately after the impact, the ship began to sink from the bow but seemed to remain stable, so the sailors did not immediately grasp the gravity of their situation. Pierce was convinced he had only scraped a shoal, and remained confident. Built in 1881 by the Castle Line, a Glaswegian shipbuilding company, the steamship was more robust than many others. The crew kept calm and assembled the passengers, trying at all costs to avoid panic. As a precaution, steam was released from the engine room to forgo any risk of the boilers exploding in case seawater would get in. The lifeboats were ready to be launched. But in less than ten minutes, the liner sank straight down, without having had time to set off a mayday call or rescue the passengers.

On the morning of June 17, when going to collect his lobster pots, Mathieu Masson, skipper of the *Couronne de Marie*, a sloop from Molène, pulled two people from the sea. Joseph Berthelé from Ushant saved a third, exhausted and chilled to the bone. They were the only survivors.

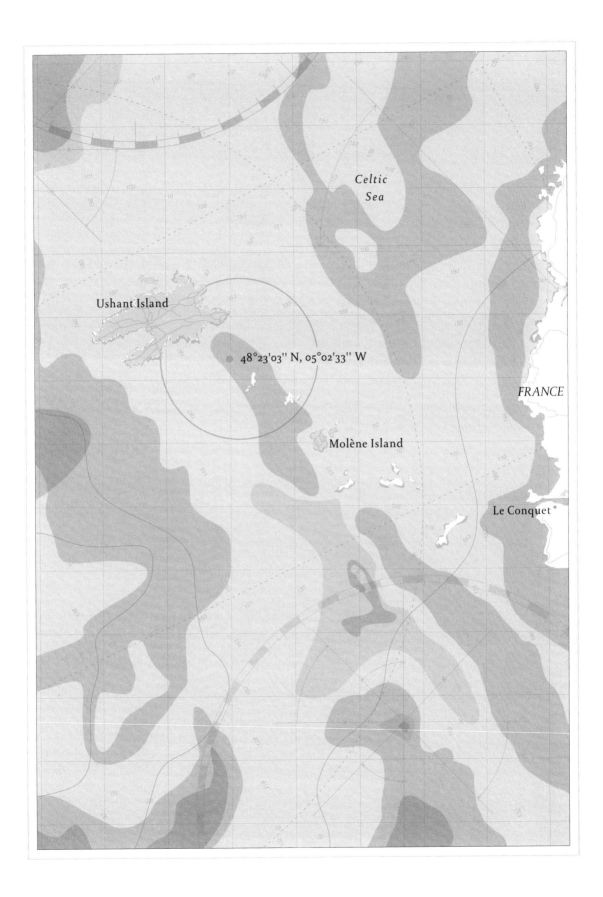

Celtic
Sea

Ushant Island

48°23'03'' N, 05°02'33'' W

Molène Island

FRANCE

Le Conquet

Almost all of the 250 people on board, including one hundred crew members, drowned. For weeks the sea continued to spit out bodies and debris. On land the victims were buried in local cemeteries, the sails of boats were cut up to serve as shrouds, cafés were turned into *chapelles ardentes* to lay out the bodies, and life was dictated by the rhythm of macabre discoveries. One family even offered their sons' and daughters'

seeing the silhouette of a woman dressed in white floating above the waves. Legend took the relay from the disaster.

In Britain there was an immense outpouring of emotion, and the press launched a national program to underwrite the cost. Queen Victoria distributed medals and gifted Molène a vermeil chalice adorned with precious stones, as well as a sundial, and financed a freshwater cistern. Ushant received the money it needed to complete the bell tower of the church of Saint-Pol-Aurélien, and the village of Ploudalmézeau was given funds to build a new dock and redevelop the port of Portsall. In 1904, the French Lighthouse Board eventually decided to improve the beaconing of the Fromveur and Ushant area by constructing the La Jument lighthouse, followed by lighthouses at Kéréon in 1907 and at Nividic in 1912. Without the shock of the loss of the SS *Drummond Castle*, none of this might have happened.

> On land the victims were buried in local cemeteries, the sails of boats were cut up to serve as shrouds, cafés were turned into *chapelles ardentes* to lay out the bodies, and life was dictated by the rhythm of macabre discoveries.

Sunday best to appropriately bury children who had died in the shipwreck. The islanders showed extraordinary dedication. At the vigil the mourners talked about occasionally hearing the ship's siren in the night and

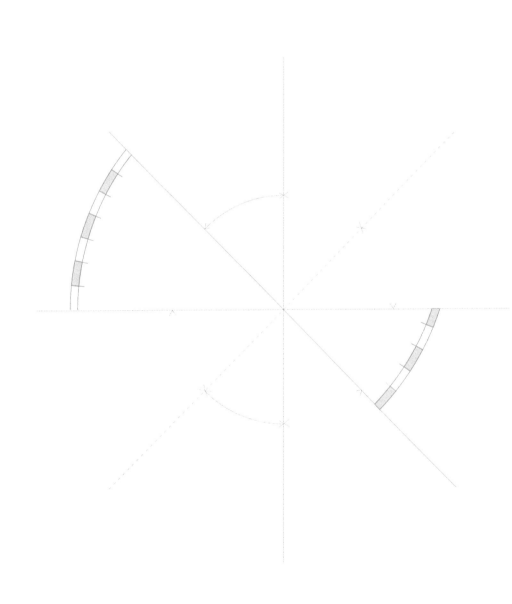

THE *SEDOV* AFFAIR

HOW TO SPOIL SEA FESTIVALS BY TRYING TO HIJACK ONE OF THE WORLD'S LARGEST SHIPS

48°23'22" N, 04°29'15" W

The arrival of the *Sedov*, a Russian four-master and the largest training ship in the world, in any port, is a delight. On July 13, 2000, while the maritime festivals of Brest and Douarnenez were in full swing, a somewhat hesitant bailiff presented himself on the *Sedov*'s gangway

> Following a decision by the Court of Brest relating to the financial dispute between Russia and a Swiss import-export company, the huge 384-foot-long (117 meter) vessel was confiscated, pure and simple.

and announced to the 176 crew—one hundred cadets from the Murmansk Naval School, fifteen students from Moscow,

the youngest of whom was only thirteen years old, and their officers—that he had come to arrest them. The man handed commander Victor Mishenyov, who did not speak French, an official document stating that following a decision by the Court of Brest relating to the financial dispute between Russia and a Swiss import-export company, the huge 384-foot-long (117 meter) vessel was confiscated, pure and simple. On board, no one had heard of this story, and it was believed to be a hoax. Yet, it was all true. In 1991, the complainant company had entered into a contract with the Kremlin to supply basic necessities in exchange for oil and gas. The contract amounted to more than $1.45 billion and specified that, in case of a dispute, the Russian state would lose its sovereign immunity and would have to fund its debt with national property. But a few months later, the USSR ceased to exist, and delivery chains were disrupted. After endless negotiations, the Swiss appealed to the international courts and obtained an injunction from the Stockholm Arbitration Court

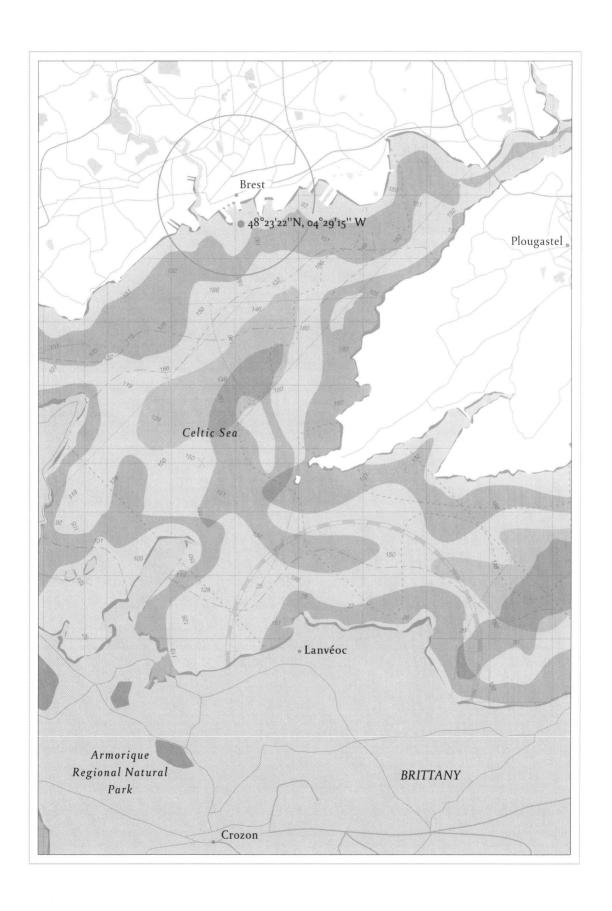

Brest

48°23'22"N, 04°29'15" W

Plougastel

Celtic Sea

Lanvéoc

Armorique
Regional Natural
Park

BRITTANY

Crozon

forcing Moscow to pay $23 million for their breach of contract. Russia appealed. But the Swedish court sentenced Russia again and increased the compensation fine by an additional $40 million. The ruling set a precedent and allowed creditors henceforth to seize any property belonging to the Russian Federation to sell it and recover what they were owed.

In France's second military port, where nearly a million visitors had come to admire one of the season's most important gatherings of historic tall ships, the organizers were caught short. The press gath-

The press gathered around the ship, which had become collateral damage of the collapse of the Soviet Union.

ered around the ship, which had become collateral damage of the collapse of the Soviet Union, the Swiss celebrated, and Moscow, which became more annoyed

with every passing day, urged Paris to immediately solve the situation. For years the *Sedov*—like the *Krusenstern* and the *Mir*, two other tall sailing ships flying the Russian flag—has been a stalwart of maritime festivals, which punctuate the seafaring calendar, and losing her would have amounted to a disaster. Under pressure, the tribunal's chairperson eventually agreed to let the ship participate in the regattas. Then the verdict was in and the confiscation was lifted. Everyone in Brest was relieved. But within an hour, the lawyers of the opposing party filed an enforcement appeal with the Rennes Court of Appeal. However, for the suspensive procedure to take effect, it had to be preceded by an appeal. But that day the prosecutor general's office in Rennes was closed, and without further ado the *Sedov* set sail. The Swiss, who could only face the facts, denounced this denial of justice coupled with a scandalous intervention by the French state and tried one last time to mobilize their lawyers. Too late, the ship had already sailed to Madeira. The plaintiffs lost a battle but not the war.

In 2001 they tried to seize two Russian air force fighter jets displayed at the Salon du Bourget, and in 2005 they tried to get hold of fifty-four impressionist masterpieces from the collection of the Pushkin Museum in Moscow exhibited at the Fondation Pierre Gianadda in Martigny, Switzerland. Without success.

For years, the *Sedov*—like the *Krusenstern* and the *Mir*, two other tall sailing ships flying the Russian flag—has been a stalwart of maritime festivals, which punctuate the seafaring calendar, and losing her would have amounted to a disaster.

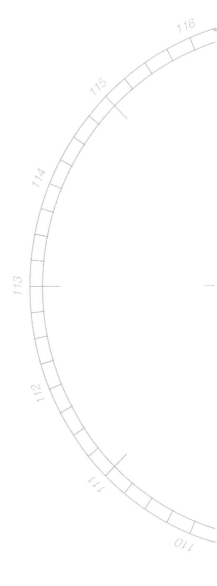

THE *DUGUAY-TROUIN*

THE VESSEL FRANCE LOST TWICE

———— ◼ ————

50°38'33" N, 01°19'20" W

She was the last French seventy-four and one of the oldest warships in the world, but France did not want her. Loaded with 450 tons of ballast and explosives, the *Duguay-Trouin* perished alone, broken up by the swell east of the Isle of Wight on December 2, 1949, after having spent more time under the flag of the British Royal Navy than under the French Tricolore. Her capture at the Battle of Cape Ortegal, off Galicia, on November 4, 1805, marked the final action of the Trafalgar campaign. That day, British rear-admiral Sir Richard Strachan put Rear-Admiral Pierre Dumanoir's French squadron out of action. In addition to the *Duguay-Trouin*, the *Mont Blanc*, the *Formidable*, and the *Scipion* fell into the hands of the British. Renamed HMS *Implacable*, the ship built between 1794 and 1801 at Rochefort fought the Russian fleet in the Baltic Sea until 1813, then took part in the blockade of the Syrian coast in 1840 and the bombardment of Alexandria. Placed in reserve in 1842, she arrived in Devonport in 1855 to serve as a training vessel. At dock, what was once "the most beautiful vessel in the Mediterranean" slowly withered and narrowly escaped demolition in 1908. Sold to a passionate millionaire, she served mainly as a dormitory for sea scouts. In 1930 the mayor of London and the Duke of York launched a joint program to underwrite the cost to restore the ship, but money was short. In June 1932 her hull was towed to Portsmouth and anchored next to the HMS *Victory*, Admiral Nelson's legendary ship. In January 1947 she was permanently decommissioned, and the Royal Navy, which was already going bankrupt over maintaining the HMS *Victory*, did not hide its predicament. The HMS *Implacable* was doomed. She became a political issue, and committees formed on both sides of the Channel to try to save her by returning her to France. Rochefort and Nantes offered to host her, but the secretary of state for the French navy refused. Amid an economic recovery, France had other priorities than the restoration of an eighteenth-century ship of the line. The director of the Musée national de la Marine tried to convince the authorities one last time but was told that "a defeated ship had no right to return to her country of origin." Her figurehead was dismantled, as was the painting at her stern and her large capstan, and the date of her death was set. On December 2, the anniversary of Emperor Napoleon's coronation, the tall ship slowly left Portsmouth Harbor to the sound of the Royal Marines playing *God Save the Queen* and the *Marseillaise*. Towed toward the open sea, she was blasted and sank to the bottom of the sea with flying colors.

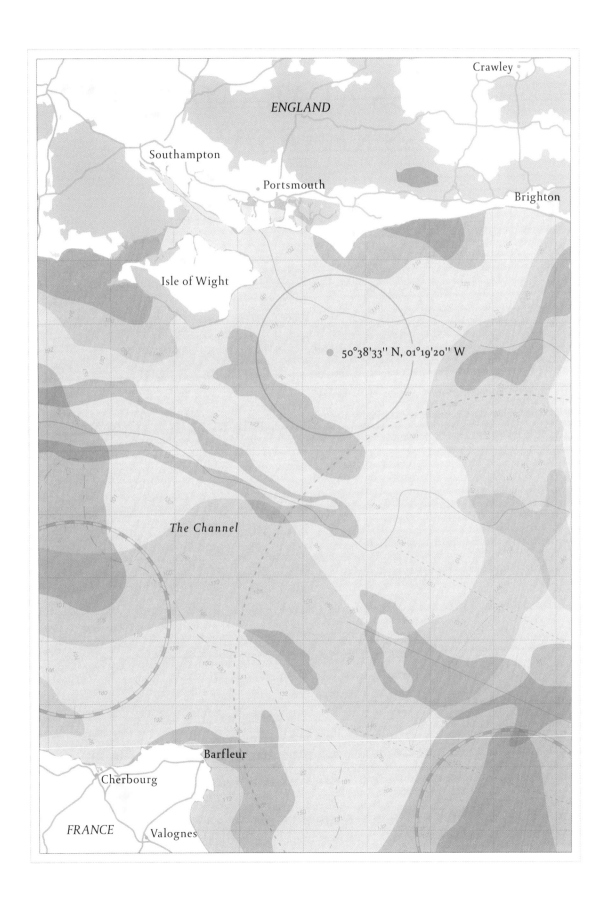

THE DUEL BETWEEN THE CSS *ALABAMA* AND USS *KEARSARGE*

THE CIVIL WAR ON TOUR IN CHERBOURG

49°38'03" N, 01°37'33" W

Legend has it that Édouard Manet was among the first to arrive as part of the crowds that gathered on June 19, 1864, on the highest points in Cherbourg and the Pointe de Querqueville to watch the duel between the Confederate privateer ship CSS *Alabama* and the Union's war sloop USS *Kearsarge*. But it seems that spectators' accounts were the main in-

> Yet, *The Battle of the Kearsarge and the Alabama*, kept in the Philadelphia Museum of Art, remains one of the best illustrations of this incredible naval episode of the Civil War.

spiration for the artist's famous painting. Yet, *The Battle of the Kearsarge and the Alabama*, kept in the Philadelphia Museum of Art, remains one of the best illus-

trations of this incredible naval episode of the Civil War.

On June 11, 1864, when the CSS *Alabama* approached the Cotentin coast after conducting a *guerre de course* over two years, the ship, under the command of Captain Raphael Semmes, was in a bad state. Its copper sheathing had suffered and its hull was in need of repairs. The unseizable Southerner, who had captured dozens of whaleboats and Unionist merchant ships, was the thorn in the side of the Northerners, and France, although neutral, was slow to give her permission to enter its naval shipyard. The diplomatic situation was all the more complicated since the *Alabama* had prisoners on board. Alerted by his consul, the representative of the United States immediately sailed USS *Kearsarge* from the Dutch port where she was stocking up on supplies, and ordered her to put away with the enemy privateer. On June 14, *Kearsarge*, under the command of Captain John Winslow, a peer of Semmes's, was in sight of the harbor of Cherbourg, and the *Alabama*, trapped, decided proudly on a counterattack. News spread throughout

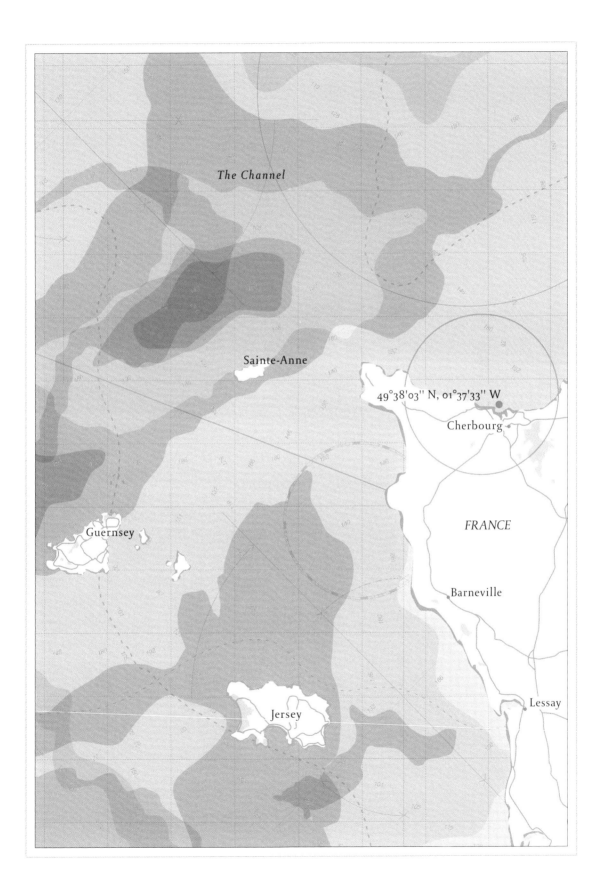

The Channel

Sainte-Anne

49°38'03'' N, 01°37'33'' W

Cherbourg

FRANCE

Guernsey

Barneville

Jersey

Lessay

Tourists flocked to the city, where everyone was betting on the *Alabama*, and street vendors, peddlers, and bookmakers filled their pockets.

France that the battle was to take place soon.

Tourists flocked to the city—taking advantage of the new railway link with Paris—where everyone was betting on the *Alabama*, and street vendors, peddlers, and bookmakers filled their pockets. On Sunday, June 19, at 9:30 a.m., the *Alabama* left the port, escorted by the imperial frigate *Couronne*, tasked with accompanying the two adversaries out of French waters. USS *Kearsarge* sailed northeast as if fleeing, then tacked and charged at the enemy. The Confederates, better armed, were the first to open fire. The cannonade could be heard for miles, and

the two ships shot tirelessly at each other. In the smoke the Unionist vessel managed to move in front of the *Alabama* to prevent it from returning to French waters. The battle lasted a little over an hour and finished in favor of *Kearsarge*. Several blows hit the Southerner at the waterline, so the *Alabama* developed a list and sank slowly from the rear, its engine underwater. To avoid a massacre, Semmes resolved to lower the flag and was among the last to abandon ship. While the privateer ship sank to the bottom of the Channel just across from the large natural harbor, the survivors were picked up and the wounded treated at the Maritime Hospital of Cherbourg. The *Alabama* lost about thirty men and USS *Kearsarge* only one man, who succumbed to his wounds. He was buried alongside two Confederates at Cherbourg Cemetery, where a monument was erected in memory of the battle. In November 1984, the French navy minesweeper *Circé* discov-

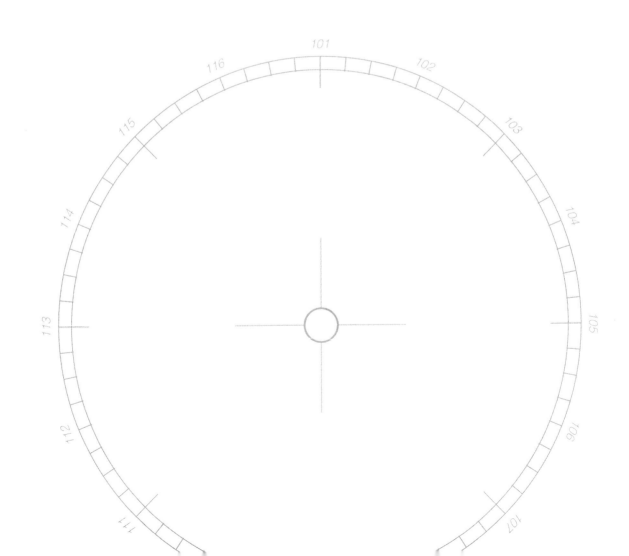

FROM THE BALTIC SEA
TO THE FAR NORTH

THE MYSTERY OF CATHERINE THE GREAT'S LOST PAINTINGS

THE TREASURE OF THE *VROUW MARIA*

———————

59°47'50" N, 21°36'05" E

Captain Lourens would have fought to the very end to save his ship. Caught in a violent storm off Finland, the *Vrouw Maria*, a 98-foot-long (30 meter), 280-ton merchant ship, had left Amsterdam on September 5, 1771, for St. Petersburg and had steered ever closer to the coast in search of shelter. But instead of leading her to salvation, her captain, lost in the maze of small islands and sandbanks of the Turku archipelago, led her straight onto the reefs. At first the impact only slightly dented the hull just below the waterline, and the damage appeared minor.

The ship was carrying about thirty canvases carefully packed in watertight rolls and signed by some of the greatest painters of the Dutch golden age.

Then one wave after another, one stronger than the next, struck her from the stern and damaged the rudder. The two-master rotated on her anchor, drifted, and hit the rocks again. For four days the crew used all their energy to work the pumps, but the black water of the Baltic Sea soon drowned the lower deck. Completely exhausted, they eventually gave up and took all they could ashore. Within minutes the *Vrouw Maria* had sunk.

At the time, its sinking made big waves, and Count Nikita Panin, the Russian foreign minister, sent diplomatic missions to the king of Sweden, the sovereign of Finland at the time, to try to recover the cargo. Because according to the logbook, the ship was carrying sugar, coffee, bales of fabrics, a few pieces of goldwork, and porcelain, but also about thirty canvases carefully packed in watertight rolls and signed by some of the greatest painters of the Dutch golden age: Paulus Potter, Gerard ter Borch, Gabriël Metsu, Isaac Koedijck, Gerrit Dou, and Philips Wouwerman. An exceptional selection formerly belonging to the famous art collector Gerrit Braamcamp, who had died a few months earlier, that had been bought at auction by Prince Dimitri Alekseyevich Gallitzin on

Fårö

Långholm

Bodö

Björkö

Baltic Sea

Jurmo

● 59°47'50'' N, 21°36'05'' E

Baltic Sea

the order of Empress Catherine II of Russia to stock the new Hermitage Museum. But the *Vrouw Maria* had vanished.

With the onset of winter, the frozen sea was covered with snow, and Panin had to eventually give up.

Forgotten for more than two centuries, her wreck was discovered by divers in 1999, a stone's throw from the small island of Jurmo, in southwest Finland, between the cities of Turku and Hanko. The research teams had high hopes for her state of conservation at an exceptional depth of 135 feet (41 meters) and very quickly set up an ambitious project to try to raise the wreck. The Baltic Sea is dark and cold but has a low salt content, so it is an ideal conservatory for organic matter, and the archeologists were convinced that the paintings—if they were still on board—would have remained in good condition. From a technical point of view, nothing was stopping the operation. But matters changed when thorny questions relating to international law arose to determine whose property the *Vrouw Maria* and her contents legally were. Since then, the site, which has been classified a "national treasure," has been monitored day and night by the Finnish authorities but has yet to reveal its secrets.

The Baltic Sea is dark and cold but has a low salt content, so it is an ideal conservatory for organic matter, and the archeologists were convinced that the paintings—if they were still on board— would have remained in good condition.

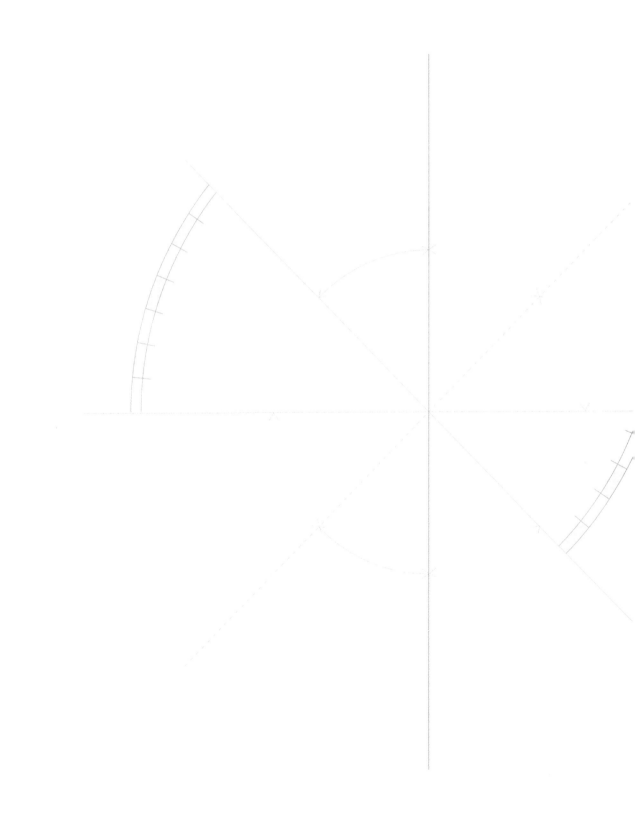

THE *VASA*, THE SHIP THAT NEVER SAILED . . .

THE PAINFUL SYMBOL OF A HISTORIC FIASCO

59°19'40" N, 18°05'29" E

There was a gentle breeze on August 10, 1628, and the *Vasa* had hoisted all her sails: three rigged each on the foremast and the mainmast, a lateen sail and a square sail on the mizzenmast, and two sails fluttering on the bowsprit. The large warship was abundant with hundreds of brightly painted sculptures, one more splendid than the next, and fired a salvo in front of the royal palace before slowly gliding across the calm sea to join the Baltic fleet. On the docks, the blue flag

It was a day of joy and bright sunshine to celebrate the regained strength of the Swedish navy, damaged by a series of defeats against Catholic Poland, which was at war with the Protestant kingdom.

with the yellow cross of the Kingdom of Sweden was fluttering in the wind. No one remembered ever having seen such a beautiful ship, and a huge crowd bid her farewell on her journey to the open sea, waving hats, handkerchiefs, and flags. It was a bright and joyous day to celebrate the regained strength of the Swedish navy, weakened by a series of defeats against Catholic Poland, which was at war with the Protestant kingdom. Taking the helm with caution, the captain set sail east, leaving the sheltered part of the harbor. The maneuver was executed perfectly. But while the crew was preparing to retrieve the guns and closing the lower gunports, a gust of wind tipped the *Vasa* portside. The sails were lowered, and the vessel of more than 200 tons and 226 feet in length (69 meters) was just straightening up when a second gust, a little stronger than the first, pushed her over again to one side. Having sailed less than a mile, the *Vasa* capsized and sank like a stone. Too heavy, too high, and not weighted enough, one of the most beautiful three-masters of her time disappeared in the depths of the port of Stockholm, taking with her about fifty sailors trapped below deck.

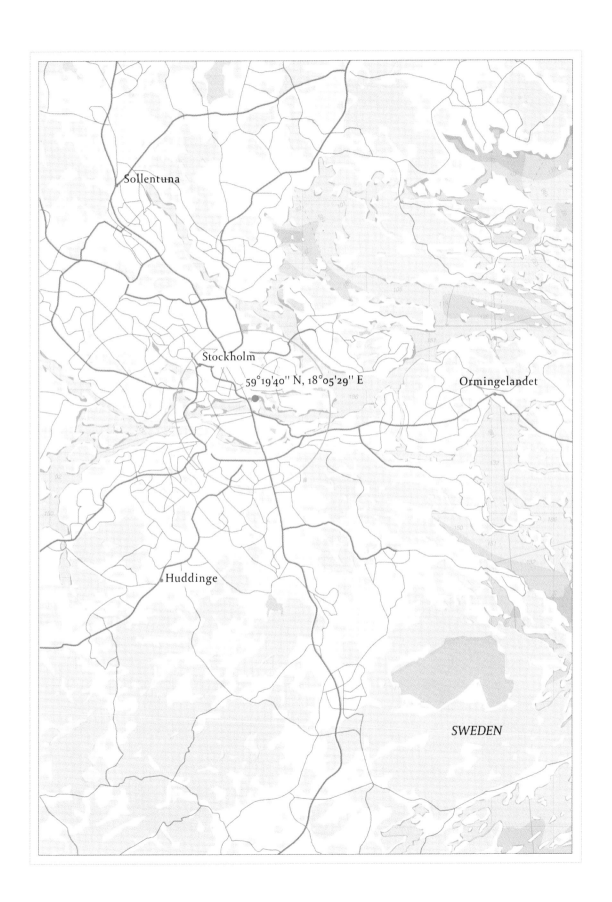

Sollentuna

Stockholm

59°19'40'' N, 18°05'29'' E

Ormingelandet

Huddinge

SWEDEN

Too heavy, too high, and not weighted enough, one of the most beautiful three-masters of her time disappeared in the depths of the port of Stockholm, taking with her about fifty sailors trapped below deck.

When he was told about the fate of his ephemeral flagship on August 27, King Gustav II Adolph wanted to find a culprit to be hanged.

But the investigation conducted by his privy council led to nothing. The shipbuilder had been dead a long time, the crew did not make any mistakes, and the shipyard had followed the plans to a T, including the fittings. Lest he himself take responsibility for the catastrophe, the sovereign was forced to accept the facts: the sinking of the *Vasa* was God's will. So be it.

In 1664, most of its sixty-four guns were recovered, and the site of the disaster, marked by a tiny dot on nautical maps, fell into oblivion until the early 1950s, when amateur archeologist Anders Franzén proposed to lift the wreck. On April 24, 1961, under the eyes of King Gustav VI Adolph, one of the descendants of the soldier king, a carved wooden head slowly emerged from the water, then a second burst through the surface. Supported by steel cables, the hull of the three-master soon appeared as a whole, practically intact. After years of careful restoration, the ship, as well as thousands of objects salvaged alongside it, has been on display at the Vasa Museum since 1990. What had been a ghost of shame lingering in the shadows at a depth of 105 feet (32 meters), the painful symbol of a historic fiasco, has since become one of the most visited tourist attractions in Scandinavia. The Swedes have turned this bitter failure into a national triumph.

THE DISAPPEARANCE OF THE HMS *EREBUS* AND *TERROR*

THE SONG PASSED ON BY THE INUIT

68°08' N, 99°15' W

Departing from Kent and the banks of the river Thames on May 19, 1845, the HMS *Erebus* and *Terror* made a brief stop in the Orkneys, in northern Scotland, before heading toward Greenland and the "open sea of the North Pole"—a putative stretch of water that the members of John Franklin's expedition hoped to reach. With reinforced hulls, 20-horsepower steam engines, and a revolutionary heating system for the crew quarters, the two Royal Navy bomb vessels had already proven themselves in Antarctica in search of the magnetic South Pole, under the helm of English explorer James Clark Ross. Planning ahead, Captain Franklin, an Arctic veteran, had three years' worth of provisions aboard: 60 tons of flour, 14 tons of beef, and 15 tons of canned meat. Some thought that Franklin, at fifty-nine years old, was too old, but he was a respected sailor. James Fitzjames, a young officer of thirty-four years, renowned thanks to his service in the Yellow Sea and his campaigns in the Mediterranean and the East, was given command of the *Erebus*, and Francis Crozier, who had already been in charge of the *Terror* during Ross's expe-

dition, took his familiar spot at the helm. Born in county Down, Northern Ireland, in 1796, he was very well qualified and had already participated in five polar expeditions. This one was his sixth, and Franklin knew he could count on him. Most of the 134 sailors and officers were English, Irish, or Scottish. Everyone knew the ins and outs of their job, but the Far North was a blank slate to them.

After sailing in convoy with the steamship HMS *Rattler* and the transport ship *Barretto Junior*, which would take five discharged men and the crew's letters back to England, the HMS *Erebus* and the *Terror* left Disko Bay, on the west coast of Greenland, in July 1845. In early August they sailed into the Baffin Sea, waiting to cross to Lancaster Sound and head toward the Northwest Passage. John Franklin was confident. His ships could advance through the ice at a speed of 4 knots, and, according to his notes, they had only 900 nautical miles to travel before finding what they were looking for. But the last people to see them were the sailors of the whalers *Enterprise* and *Prince of Wales*. No one else would see them alive.

66

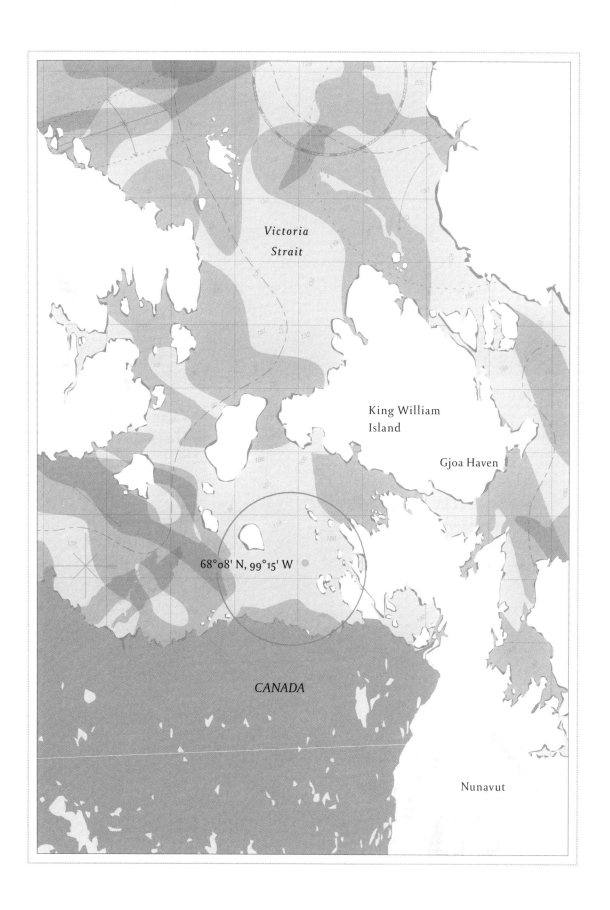

Victoria
Strait

King William
Island

Gjoa Haven

68°08' N, 99°15' W

CANADA

Nunavut

In 1848, under pressure from the public and Jane Griffin, Franklin's second wife, the British Admiralty offered a reward of 20,000 pounds sterling to whoever could give them information as to their whereabouts, and sent out three research expeditions at once. The first, led by naturalist John Richardson and explorer John Rae, would take the land route along the Mackenzie River to the river mouth. The other two would travel by sea from the Canadian Arctic Archipelago through Lancaster Sound and along the Pacific coast. But there was not a trace of the two ships. The affair grew to international proportions, and, from 1850, about fifty vessels took turns in search of Franklin and his men. But the more time passed, the slimmer the chances of finding them. On the east coast of Beechey Island, three graves were discovered in which sailors from the *Erebus* and the *Terror* had been buried. Then, while exploring the Boothia Peninsula, south of Somerset Island, John Rae met with Inuit who assured him that about forty white men had died of starvation near the mouth of the Back River in present-day Nunavut. Other seal hunters, who had to witness their agony without being able to help, gave Rae several silver forks and spoons later identified as belonging to James Fitzjames, Francis Crozier, and John Franklin. In 1855, pieces of wood engraved with "Erebus" and "Mr. Stanley"—the name of the ship's surgeon—were found on Montreal Island in the Chantrey Inlet, where the Back River meets the sea. All hope had been lost, and on March 31, 1854, Britain officially declared the death in service of the members of the Franklin Expedition.

But Lady Franklin did not give up the fight and managed to convince explorer Francis Leopold McClintock to resume the search. His ship, the schooner *Fox*, was purchased by public subscription and left Aberdeen on July 2, 1857. In May 1859, under a cairn on King William Island, his men discovered two messages by Crozier and Fitzjames written on the same sheet of paper. The first, dated May 28, 1847, was reassuring. After having circumnavigated Cornwallis Island and stopping on Beechey Island from 1845 to 1846, the HMS *Erebus* and the *Terror* wintered in the ice off the northwest coast of King William Island.

"All well," the message read. But the second, written eleven months later on April 25, 1848, was frightening. The ships had remained trapped on an ice floe in an area where the ice was not very mobile and rarely melts during the summer months, so the crew had to abandon ship. Twenty-four officers and sailors died, including Franklin, who passed away on June 11, 1847. Francis Crozier had taken command, and the survivors were preparing to leave on foot on April 26, 1848, toward the Back River. Farther down the south coast, the search troops found a skeleton still dressed in shredded rags, then a little farther west a lifeboat containing two bodies and an incredible amount of abandoned useless equipment. Between 1860 and 1880, further expeditions south of the island found more burial sites and human remains. The Inuit would tell what they saw to whoever was prepared to listen: all of Franklin's men had died one after the other of starvation, cold, and disease. But when native people recounted that some of the crew ended up eating one another, most Europeans refused to believe them. However, analyses carried out on the bones of the expeditions' victims in the 1980s revealed unequivocal traces of cannibalism, as well as vitamin C deficiencies and abnormally high levels of lead. Dozens of songs passed down by the Inuit from generation to generation described the ordeal of the men of the Franklin Expedition, these ghosts with emaciated faces and "hard, dry and black" mouths, but for years no one took them seriously. In 2014 a new search campaign was carried out, and on September 7, 2014, in the Victoria Strait, near Cambridge Bay, some 186 miles (300 kilometers) from King William Island, the HMS *Erebus* was formally identified using a remote-controlled underwater vehicle. Two years later, on September 13, 2016, the HMS *Terror* was recovered, perfectly preserved, by teams of the Arctic Research Foundation. At the last moment, following the advice of Sammy Kogvik, an Indigenous crew member who recalled seeing a large piece of wood sticking out of the ice, the captain of the research vessel changed course and discovered the wreck. The ship rested at a depth of 79 feet (24 meters) southwest of King William Island, at Terror Bay, about 62 miles (100 kilometers) north of the *Erebus*. Someone had finally listened to the Inuit call.

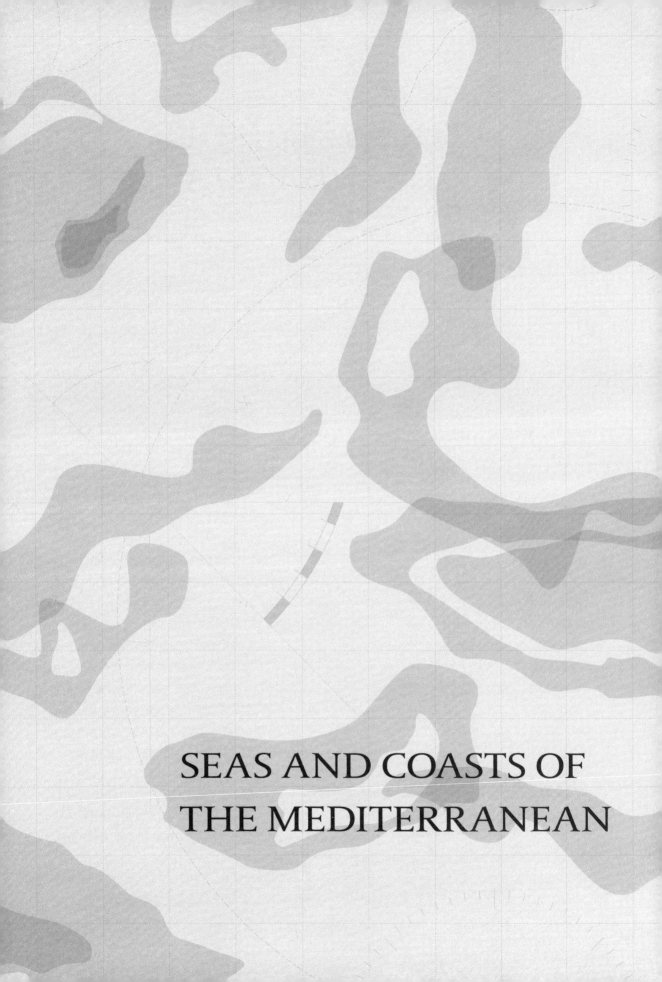

SEAS AND COASTS OF
THE MEDITERRANEAN

THE WRECK OF THE *GIRAGLIA*

THE ETERNAL RAGE OF THE *LIBECCIO*

43°01'05" N, 09°24'24" E

The scene is bright and peaceful when divers plunge to the remains of this ship lost with all hands in the first century CE off the island of Giraglia, at the tip of Cap Corse. In fine weather, in front of the ashen backdrop, the Neptune seagrass is reflecting the sunlight, these thin jade-green blades that undulate in the current. There is barely anything else to distract the eye. The wreck, which has been studied in depth by the teams of archeologists Martine Sciallano and Sabrina Marlier, is nothing out of the ordinary. The remains of her load—a dozen huge cisterns, *dolia* that can accommodate 440 gallons (2,000 liters) of oil or wine, earthenware jars of a more modest size, and some amphorae whose largest fragments are just about the size of a hand—rest at 66 feet (20 meters) in depth about 1,640 feet (500 meters) from the coast. Under the sand and sediment, some elements of the ship's ribs and keel miraculously survived. Thanks to a stamp discovered on the neck of one of the *dolia*, it is assumed that this heavy sailboat of 66 feet (20 meters) in length and 20 feet (6 meters) in width was flying the flag of the Pirani of Minturnes, shipowners operating from the southern Lazio region, between Rome and Naples, and that part of her cargo of wine probably came from Tarragona, Spain.

No treasure has been recovered. No epic battle caused her loss, and history has retained neither her name nor that of the men who died on board while trying to reach the port of Ostia, on the left bank of the mouth of the Tiber River. Were they sailing at night, along the coast, in a hurry to deliver their cargo to the Pirani, who had promised them a reward? Did they not notice the sea getting rough and the sky darkening? Yet, the *dolia* very quickly broke from their ties, rolling in all directions, breaking the amphorae and smashing the planking. Shattered, some spilled all the wine they contained, further destabilizing the ship. The anchor, discovered a little farther west, may have been dropped in an emergency to try to reduce her speed. But within just a few minutes, everything had toppled over. So why linger here at all? Probably because the *libbecio* hit it from the stern, this violent southwesterly wind that still blows here today, centuries later, without offering a truce or respite. Even big ferries that now cross the Mediterranean avoid facing it. The mystery of the shipwreck is often more fascinating than the disaster itself. In this case, it is this disturbing proximity that sends a shiver down our spines.

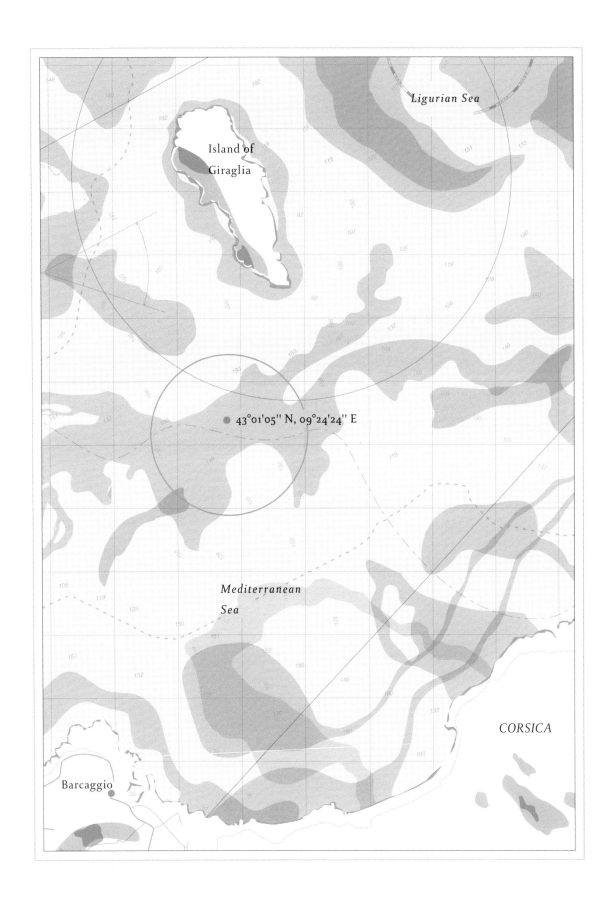

Ligurian Sea

Island of
Giraglia

● 43°01'05" N, 09°24'24" E

Mediterranean
Sea

CORSICA

Barcaggio

THE *GRAND SAINT ANTOINE*

WHEN RATS LEAVE THE SHIP TOO QUICKLY

43°17'47" N, 05°22'12" E

The day the *Grand Saint Antoine*, a store-ship loaded with precious fabrics from the Levant, arrived in sight of the Frioul archipelago on May 25, 1720, the great fair of Beaucaire was only weeks away, and the shipowners were prepared to do anything to avoid her being placed in a long quarantine. But the endeavor had gotten off to a bad start. A passenger who had embarked in Tripoli died along with

> In Marseille, where people were dying in the streets, the disease had already claimed more than thirty thousand victims and was now spreading to Provence and the Languedoc.

eight sailors, including the ship's surgeon, struck down by a mysterious illness. People feared the plague, but nobody dared to utter the word. The ship's health warrant, signed in Cyprus, was no longer valid, and that issued by the authorities of the Italian port of Livorno, who had attributed the deaths to "an evil, pestilent fever," was more than dubious. However, the aldermen of Marseille let themselves be convinced, and the cargo was unloaded on the docks. Usually, most vessels were thoroughly inspected in the small port of the island of Pomègues and their crew placed under the supervision of the health stewards at the lazaret of Arenc. But nothing went as planned, and the *Grand Saint Antoine* remained in isolation for just twenty days. On June 20, the plague-carrying fleas who had infested the rats on board spread around the city, and the sick started to drop like flies. Regent Philippe d'Orléans ordered the ship to be burned, but his orders were not carried out until September 25 and 26. Far too late. In Marseille, where people were dying in the streets, the disease had already claimed more than thirty thousand victims and was now spreading to Provence and the Languedoc. In hindsight, scientists today believe that the plague not only hid in

74

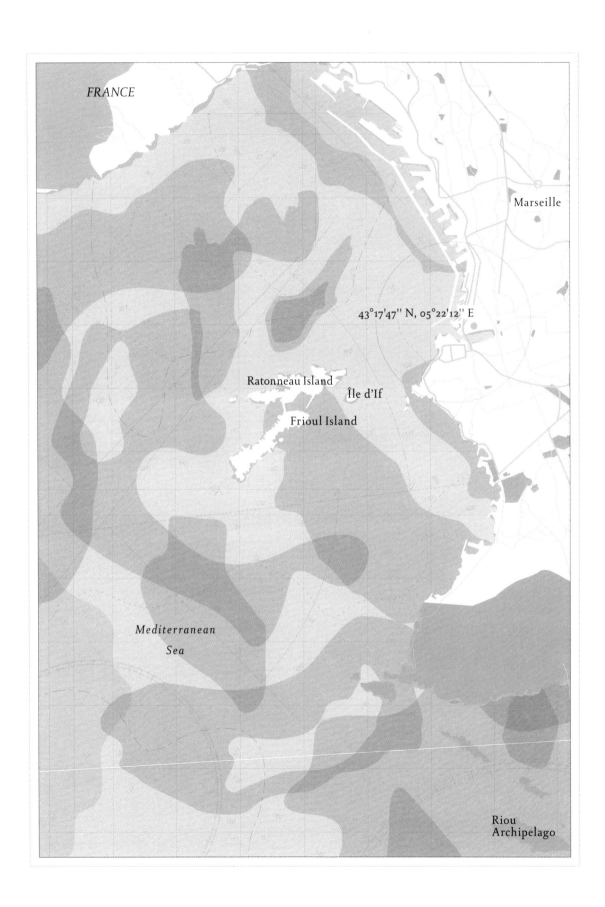

FRANCE

Marseille

43°17'47'' N, 05°22'12'' E

Ratonneau Island

Île d'If

Frioul Island

Mediterranean
Sea

Riou
Archipelago

the holds of the *Grand Saint Antoine* but also originated from a local resurgence of the *Yersinia pestis* bacillus.

The same bacterium had already devastated Europe in 1347, four centuries earlier. Back then, the epidemic had also begun in Marseille. On November 1, 1347, on All Saints' Day—the day before the Day of the Dead—one of the Genoese galleys that had fled the siege of Kaffa, in Crimea, moored at the port with the

In the first weeks the disease spread at an average of 46 miles per day and sowed desolation in overcrowded cities.

plague on board. In the first weeks the disease spread at an average of 46 miles (75 kilometers) per day and sowed desolation in overcrowded cities, taking advantage of trade routes, especially rivers, and maritime networks. After Marseille, Avignon was hit in January 1348, followed by Montpellier and Béziers. In February the plague arrived in Narbonne, in early March in Carcassonne, and in late March in Perpignan. In June the epidemic reached Bordeaux, from where it spread to England. During the summer it appeared in Rouen, then in Pontoise and Saint-Denis. On August 20, 1348, the plague broke out in Paris, where five hundred people died every day. In December 1348 it had invaded all of southern Europe and was raging from Greece to southern England. Between 1348 and 1352, between 30 and 50 percent of the population of Europe, or about forty-five million people, were killed by the Black Death.

And as if that were not enough, in 1423, in the midst of the War of Succession between the House of Anjou and the House of Aragon over the question of who owned the Kingdom of Naples, Marseille was ransacked and burned to the ground. Stoked by a strong wind, the fire lasted three days. The Aragonese systematically plundered the port houses, destroyed

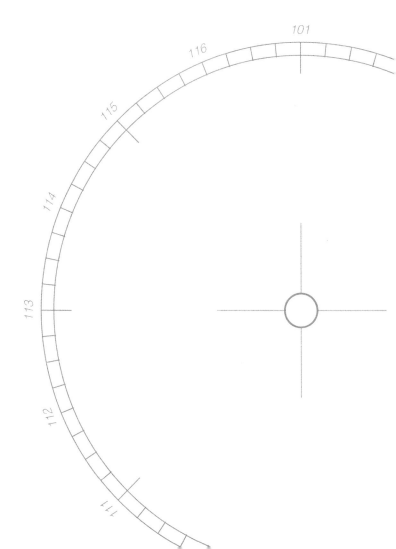

THE AGONY OF
THE *SÉMILLANTE*

THE TEARS SHED BY ALPHONSE DAUDET

41°20' N, 09°15' E

"Since the mistral the other night has cast us up on the Corsican coast, allow me to tell you a dreadful tale of the sea, which fishermen down there talk about in guarded voices when evening comes, and about which chance furnished me with some very strange pieces of information" (translated by Frederick Davies). When Alphonse Daudet published "L'agonie de la *Sémillante*" in the newspaper *L'Événement* on October 7, 1866, a little over ten years had passed since the frigate sank. But the memory of those missing still haunted the Second Empire. Leaving Toulon on February 14, 1855, to supply the allied forces fighting the Russians in Crimea, her crew was preparing for an unprecedented crossing. The first planned stopover was Constantinople, and the sailors were already looking forward to strolling through its lanes and its large bazaar. But the ship encountered severe weather off Sardinia, and her captain, in an attempt to heave to the wind, decided to go through the Strait of Bonifacio near the Lavezzi Islands, an area renowned for its shoals and reefs. The sky looked ominous and the sea was becoming increasingly stormy. On February 15, the gusts were so strong that many roofs in the town of Bonifacio were blown off, and one house collapsed on its inhabitants. In an attempt to appease the hurricane, Abbot Rocca blessed the sea in the presence of a handful of his congregation with a fragment of the True Cross, a precious relic kept in a small church on Saint-Dominique Street. In vain. The storm only doubled in strength. There was no telling whether it was day or night anymore. In the backwash, the lighthouse keeper at La Testa thought he could see a vessel in distress. "Suddenly," writes Daudet, "a fearsome crunching crack, a cry, one single cry, one immense cry, outstretched arms, clutching hands, and in all those frightened eyes the vision of death passes like a flash of lightning." Pushed by furious west-southwesterly winds, the *Sémillante* steered too far north and smashed at full speed into the rocky shallows despite it being marked by a buoy. There were no survivors. On February 18 the current carried the first corpses to the shore, though of the 773 sailors and soldiers on board, the sea surrendered only 560.

"Poor *Sémillante*! . . . the sea had broken her at one blow. . . . As for the men, nearly all were disfigured, horribly mutilated . . . it was pitiful to see them, lying in groups, clutching each other, in clusters. . . . We found the captain in full uniform, . . . ; and in one corner, . . . a little cabin boy with his eyes open . . . we thought he was still alive; but no, it had been ordained that not one should escape!" Sailors and soldiers, officers and high-ranking military staff—they all rest together now in the two cemeteries on the Lavezzi Islands.

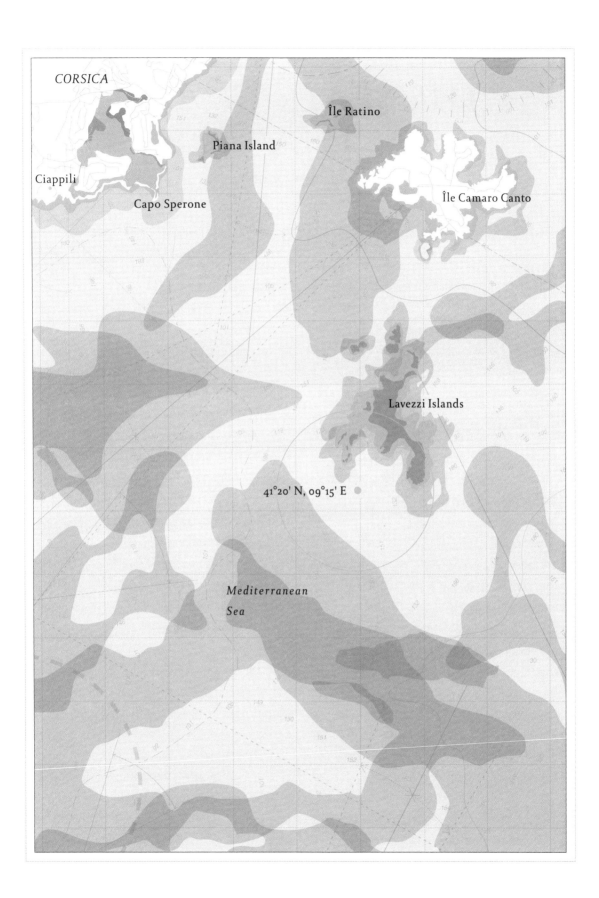

CORSICA

Île Ratino

Piana Island

Ciappili

Capo Sperone

Île Camaro Canto

Lavezzi Islands

41°20' N, 09°15' E

Mediterranean
Sea

THE *BEATRICE* AND THE PHARAOH

WHEN THE MYSTERIES OF THE SEA MEET THOSE OF ANCIENT EGYPT

31°11'40'' N, 29°52'20'' E

When the English 224-ton brig *Beatrice* left the port of Alexandria for Liverpool, she was transporting in her hold 100 tons of cotton bales and a strange piece of cargo: the enormous basalt sarcophagus of Pharaoh Menkaure, a 3-ton monolith found by Major General Vyse, who decided to donate it to the British Museum. A soldier and Egyptologist, Richard William Howard Vyse was no unknown quantity. We owe him the discovery of the engraved cartouche of King Khufu inside the Great Pyramid of Giza, for example. But years spent as a cavalry officer seem to have left their mark, and he was said to have been more of an adventurer than a scientist— to the extent that some criticize his rushed, even-ruthless exploration methods, especially his use of gunpowder to open a passage in the walls of a burial chamber.

On July 30, 1837, accompanied by engineer John Shae Perring, the major general managed to penetrate from the north side into the smallest of the three pyramids of the Giza complex. By torchlight, Vyse discovered two chambers, one on top of the other. In the first he immediately recognized the wooden sarcophagus of Khufu's grandson, whose bones lay scattered in the dust amid debris and broken wood. The Englishman was not the first

to desecrate Menkaure's tomb. The grave had already been looted, and there was not much left for the taking. But in the other burial chamber just below, archeologists discovered a magnificent basalt sarcophagus. Empty and void of any inscription, it was decorated with carved motifs in the style of a palace facade. An exceptional piece that Vyse wanted to take with him at all cost. Nothing could stop him. Neither the granite walls that lined the corridors and that he had dismantled nor its transport to Alexandria, and even less its illegal import into England without the consent of the administration of pasha Muhammad Ali. But this treasure from the Fourth Dynasty would never reach its destination. In their *Loss and Casualty Book*, Lloyd merely notes that on Thursday, January 31, 1839, the *Beatrice* "sailed from Alexandria 20th Sept. & from Malta, 13th October for Liverpool, & has not since been heard of." A wreck was reported near Cartagena on October 30, 1838, but information is scarce. Had the brig become the victim of an act of piracy? Or did it sink in a storm somewhere off the coasts of Portugal or Spain? No one will ever know. Nearly two centuries after its discovery, the mystery of the disappearance of Menkaure's sarcophagus has yet to be solved.

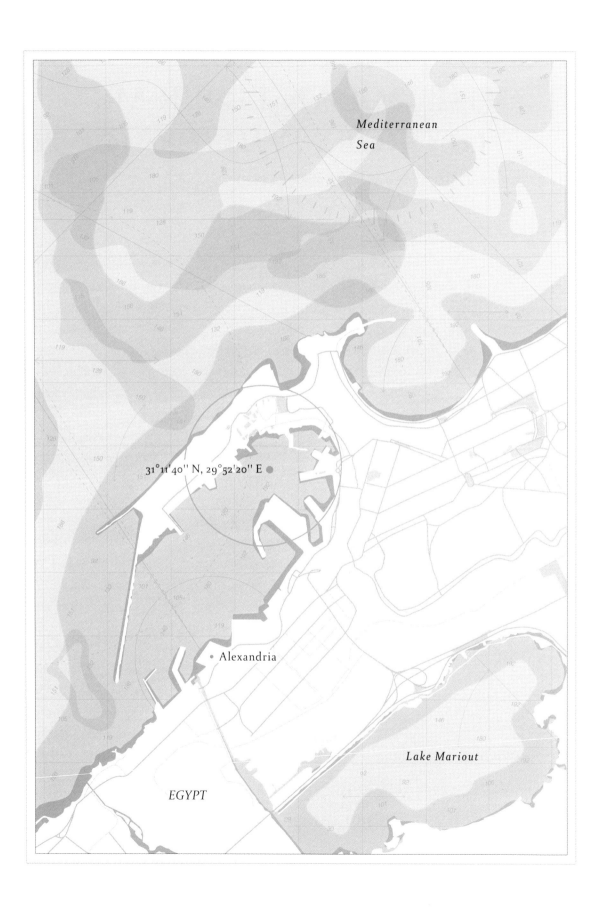

Mediterranean
Sea

31°11'40'' N, 29°52'20'' E

Alexandria

Lake Mariout

EGYPT

THE FIRE ON THE OCEAN LINER MS *GEORGES PHILIPPAR*

BUT WHO COULD HAVE RESENTED ALBERT LONDRES THAT MUCH?

12°60'05'' N, 51°16'12'' E

With his hands in his pockets, Albert Londres takes in the fresh evening air one last time and lingers on deck of the ocean liner MS *Georges Philippar* before returning to his cabin. The lights of the Cape Guardafui lighthouse sparkle in the distance on the port side, and the night of May 15 to 16, 1932, promises to be mild. The party to celebrate Pentecost is over, and the famous journalist, embarked in Shanghai, can finally relax. After having churned out one article after another on the Sino-Japanese War for months, he had secretly worked on an "explosive" dossier. Was he investigating Japanese expansion plans? Or researching the links between the Chinese Triad and opium traffickers? Or did he discover an unexpected involvement of the Bolsheviks? Albert Londres evaded the question, but everyone was expecting to read a report along the lines of those uncompromising pieces he had written about the penal colonies of Guyana and so-called lunatic asylums.

Nearly everything aboard the MS *Georges Philippar* is brand new, since the ship is on the return leg of her first commercial journey. The Messageries Maritimes shipping company was thinking big and had respected the latest boating-safety regulations to a T. The 17,359-ton ship, 561 feet (171 meters) in length, had eight watertight bulkheads and sixteen lifeboats meeting the standards of the time. Thanks to its diesel engines, it reached speeds of 16 knots. During her maiden voyage from January 20 to 26, 1932, from Saint-Nazaire to Marseille via Lisbon and Ceuta, the crew got to know her, but some superstitious sailors were a little anxious. Contrary to the usual practice of a ship bearing the name of someone to be honored after their death, the *Georges*

> Contrary to the usual practice of a ship bearing the name of someone to be honored after their death, the *Georges Philippar* was named after the president of the Messageries Maritimes shipping company, who was very much alive.

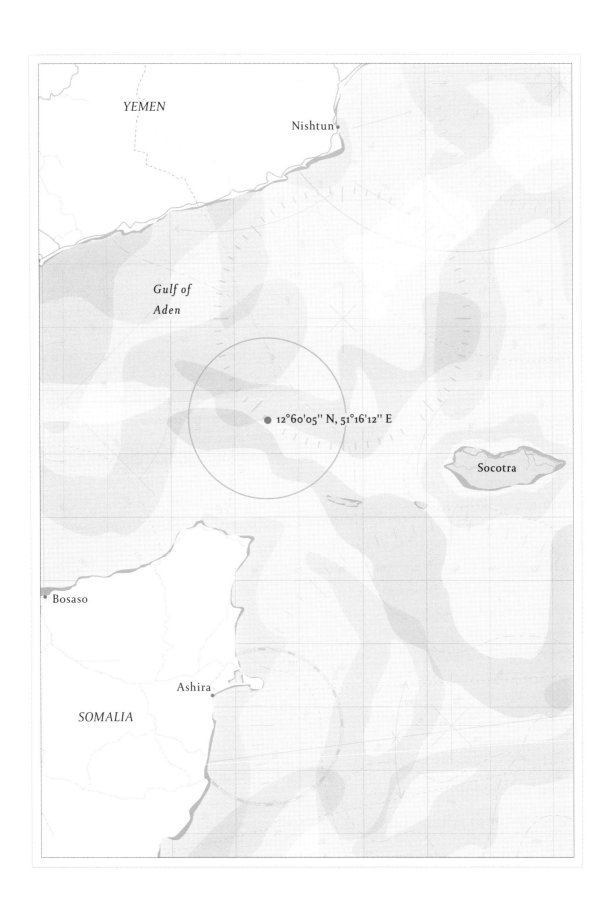

YEMEN

Nishtun •

Gulf of
Aden

● 12°60'05" N, 51°16'12" E

Socotra

Bosaso •

Ashira •

SOMALIA

Philippar was named after the president of the Messageries Maritimes shipping company, who was very much alive.

Their uneasiness was reinforced by a worrying succession of electrical-voltage problems and short circuits. But the shipowner was not worried, and the liner left Marseille as planned on February 26, 1932, bound for the Far East. Around 2:00 a.m., off the coast of Aden, a passenger bothered by an unpleasant smell of burnt rubber noticed smoke escaping from cabin number 6 on deck D and sounded the alarm. Very quickly the watch officer alerted the captain and tried to extinguish the flames with a fire extinguisher. But the disaster took its course. The fire spread with unprecedented speed. In the passageways and cabins the lights went out and the flames devoured the floors and partitions. The captain stopped the engines and decided to close the watertight doors, trapping some of the pas-

Of the 767 people on board, fifty-two went missing, among them Albert Londres.

sengers on deck D, who would burn alive or suffocate. Others managed to leave the ship in the lifeboats and were picked up by a Soviet cargo boat, the *Sovietskaia Neft*, and by the English vessels *Contractor* and *Mahsud*, before being transferred onto the *André Lebon*, which had diverted from its course due to the disaster.

At 8:35 a.m. the rescue mission was completed. In the distance, the MS *Georges Philippar* was nothing more than a burning line hovering over the water. The abandoned wreck continued to burn for three days, and on the night of May 19 to 20, after drifting more than 150 miles north, she eventually sank to a depth of 1.2 miles (2,000 meters). The superb white liner spent a total of only eighty days at sea. Of the 767 people on board, fifty-two went missing, among them Albert Londres. After the confusion of the first few days was over, when there was still hope of finding him among the survivors, eyewitnesses confirmed his disappearance. In *Le Figaro*, Monsieur Julien, an engineer at the municipal services, recounted what he saw on the night of the tragedy.

"When I left my cabin, fleeing the fire, I very clearly heard screams from the cabin occupied by Monsieur Albert Londres: 'Help! Save me!' After the horror of the first few hours and the disarray into which these tragic events had plunged us, I thought that Monsieur Albert Londres, who had probably used the electric lock to shut his cabin door, had not been able to reopen it when the fire broke out. It is a simple assumption I am proposing here, but I cannot explain why he was unable to get out of his cabin. There was also the porthole through which he could have easily escaped. Why did he not leave his cabin that way? I do not know what to think."

In the following day's edition, a second testimony, by Maurice Sadorge, one of the officers of the *Georges Philippar*, provides a possible explanation. "I was on the lifeboat deck when I heard calls from one of the luxury cabins on the deck immediately below and saw a passenger climbing out through the porthole and calling for help. It was, as I know now, Monsieur Albert Londres. I tossed him a water hose, one of those long canvas hoses that are used every morning to wash down the deck and must be used in case of a fire to fight back the flames. Monsieur Albert Londres grabbed this water hose, slipped out of the cabin, and began to pull himself up with the force of his arms, to reach the lifeboat deck. I thought him to be in safety, so I went to the rescue of the children and women, who, gathered on the upper deck, were worried and did not know what to do. We crew members helped evacuate them at the stern. But the fire hose that Monsieur Albert Londres had been holding on to tore, probably already scourged by the flames coming from the first-class deck, and he must have fallen into the sea."

However, none of these accounts answer the question everyone is asking: Was the fire of the ocean liner MS *Georges Philippar* an accident or a crime? The sudden disappearance of the famous reporter seemed suspicious, to the extent that some even assume a conspiracy to prevent him from revealing what he had seen in China. Although investigations quickly confirmed that the disaster was caused by an electrical fault, the strange death of the couple who had traveled with him, the Lang-Willars, when the plane that was taking them home crashed a few days later, reinforced the hypothesis of a plot. But no evidence was ever found.

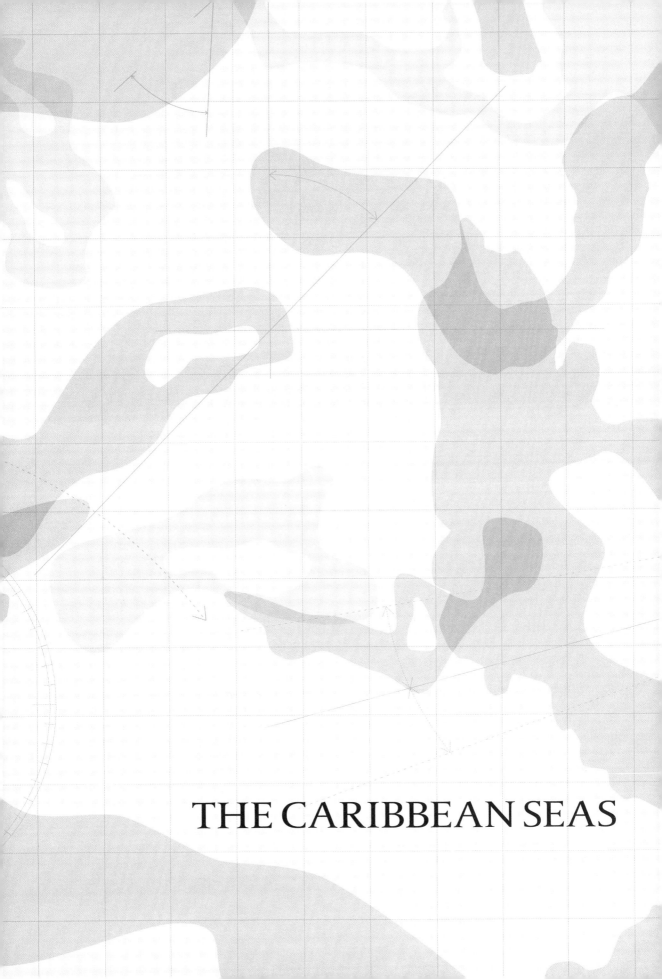

THE CARIBBEAN SEAS

THE TREASURE OF THE *NUESTRA SEÑORA DE LAS MARAVILLAS*

HOW TO MAKE THE WRECK OF A GALLEON A GENUINE EMERALD AND GOLD MINE

25°04'59" N, 77°18'49" W

Because of their location on the route that galleons took back from the New World, places such as the West Indies and the Caribbean Islands have always attracted treasure hunters. The market for lost treasures is profitable and the wrecks are numerous. Between the sixteenth and seventeenth centuries, a third of the ships of the Spanish treasure fleet, the West Indies Fleet, was taken by corsairs and pirates, sunk or shipwrecked on the reefs by cyclones, and never made it back to Spain. Despite these heavy losses, the Casa de Contratación,

> Every time a ship sank, many captains sought permission to recover anything of value.

which, until 1790, had the monopoly on maritime trade between American ports and the Iberian Peninsula, did not change its ways of conducting business. Arriving from various destinations beyond Santo Domingo,

the ships would always meet in Havana to jointly return their cargo to the Spanish kingdom. The rhythm was always the same, and it meant that up to forty galleons could navigate in convoy. Although this system served to put off enemies, if a single ship got into trouble it could delay all the others, and when the terrible tropical storms unleashed, an entire fleet could disappear with all hands.

Every time a ship sank, many captains sought permission to recover anything of value, from the cannons to the dishes. Some procured these legally, others by different means. With the help of a diving bell, in use since the late sixteenth century, at least two people could descend to a depth of about 33 feet (10 meters) for a few minutes. Accidents were not uncommon, and many died trying to grab a handful of gold coins scattered a little too far away in the sand. In 1690, physicist Edmund Halley perfected the system and equipped the device with a tighter lead coating and barrels containing air reserves. From then on, a team made up of two or three men was able to descend up to 66 feet (20 meters) below the surface and stay for a little over an

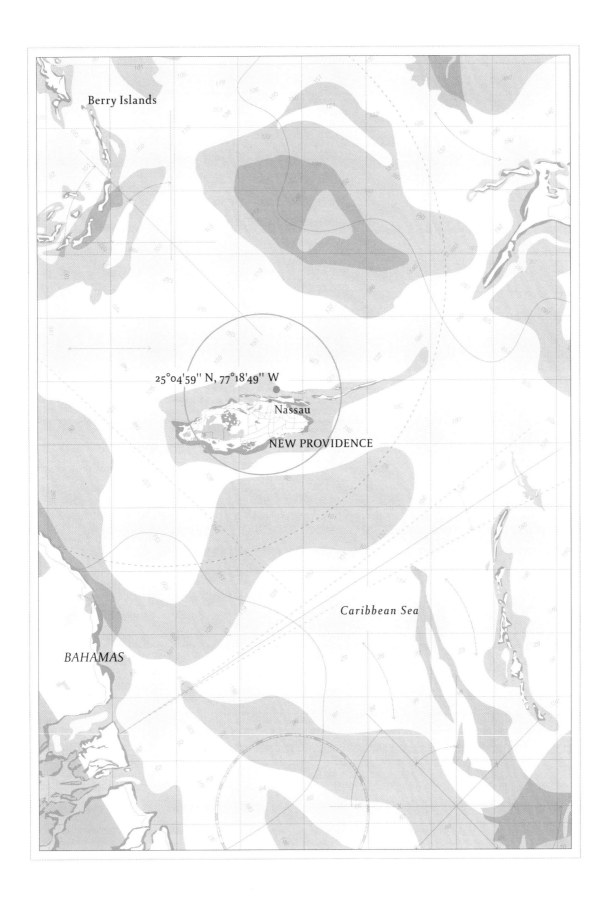

Berry Islands

25°04'59'' N, 77°18'49'' W

Nassau

NEW PROVIDENCE

Caribbean Sea

BAHAMAS

hour. Later, in 1715, John Lethbridge invented one of the first deep-sea diving suits. Consisting of a barrel equipped with oiled leather sleeves through which to pass one's arms and a porthole for observation, it allowed greater mobility, though it did not have an external air supply. Its applicability nevertheless remained limited, and most wrecks, such as that of the *Nuestra Señora de las Maravillas*, were only partially accessible. Discovered in 1972 by treasure hunter Robert Marx, the ship had run aground in shallow waters on a sandbank in the Bahamas. Weighing 900 tons and powerfully armed, this galleon formed the rearguard of a convoy that, rumor has it, was attacked

agena on August 22 after an uneventful crossing. With their precious cargo stowed in the holds, they then sailed to Havana, where they loaded up on sugar, cocoa, tobacco, and other goods. On January 1, 1656, the flotilla set off for Cádiz. Three days into the journey, another galleon accidentally rammed the *Nuestra Señora de las Maravillas*. Unable to stop the leak in the open sea, the crew headed east in search of a shoal and deliberately stranded there. Of the 650 people on board, only forty-five survived. The Spaniards managed to recover sixteen cannons, a few dozen silver ingots, and some gold coins. Despite several attempts being made, three-quarters of the cargo was lost, apparently including a life-size statue of the Virgin and Child in solid gold. Three centuries later, in the late 1980s, after lengthy discussions with the Bahamian authorities, American Herbert Humphreys succeeded in obtaining a concession for the site of the shipwreck, which he exploited just like a mine.

> Despite several attempts being made, three-quarters of the cargo was lost, apparently including a life-size statue of the Virgin and Child in solid gold.

by English privateers. Departing from Spain for the Caribbean Islands on July 10, 1654, the vessels she escorted arrived in Cart-

From the very first campaign, his divers brought up ingots, gold and silver coins, and precious jewels, including a stunning cross set with emeralds intended for the queen of Spain. However, the extent of their discoveries and the real amount of the recovered treasure remain a mystery. Was it a million dollars? A billion, even? No one really knows. Especially since only a part of the galleon has truly been explored. But whom to believe? The world of wreck hunters is often as murky as the waters they explore.

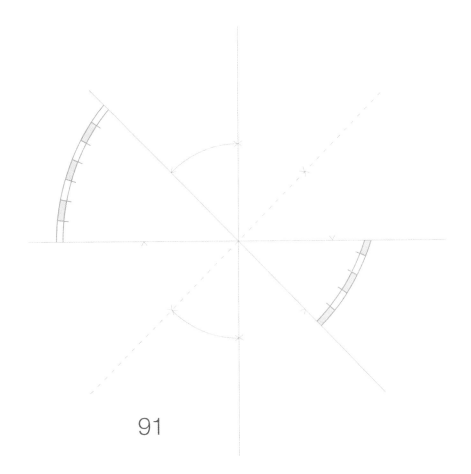

ADMIRAL D'ESTRÉES'S SHATTERED FLEET

CURAÇAO'S SIN OF PRIDE

11°58'48" N, 67°39'26" W

Having been appointed a French army *maréchal de camp* at twenty-five years of age and lieutenant general at thirty-three, Count Jean II d'Estrées was one of those high-born gentlemen of the ancien régime who obtained a command at sea without ever having been a sailor. And when he joined the ranks of his cousin, the Duke of Beaufort, who was already an accomplished master at navigation, he knew the strongholds of Flanders and the danger of the Spanish army *tercios* much better than the

> His officers were initially wary of his heated and exuberant character but were eventually forced to recognize his skills.

great military ports of the French kingdom. His officers were initially wary of his heated and exuberant character but were eventually forced to recognize his skills. Appointed first vice admiral of the Flotte du Ponant in 1669, he faced the English in the West Indies, then fought battles in the Mediterra-

nean, where he defeated the dey of Algiers. During the Franco-Dutch War (1672–78), he was promoted to commander in chief of the French squadron and only ever dreamed of battles and seeing enemy ships up in flames. His command kept enemies at bay. But in June 1674, Dutch troops managed to land at Belle-Île-en-Mer and plundered Noirmoutier. At Versailles the affair caused a scandal, and Jean d'Estrées narrowly escaped dismissal. His hatred of the Dutch became increasingly visceral. In October 1676 he left Brest with four fifty-gun ships, four frigates, and the firm intention of retaking Cayenne, which had just fallen into the hands of the United Provinces. On December 21 he achieved just that. On February 20 the French fleet headed for the Caribbean island of Tobago, toward New Walcheren Bay, where the enemy's ships laid at anchor. But d'Estrées's attack failed, and what remained of his fleet fled to Grenada.

He returned to France in July 1677, rearmed his fleet on November 1, and—as he did in

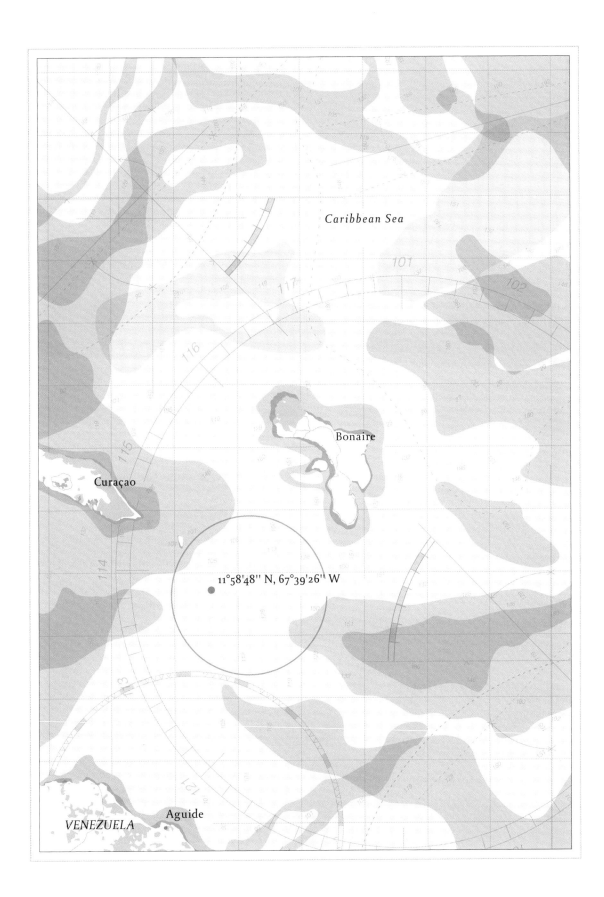

Caribbean Sea

Bonaire

Curaçao

11°58'48'' N, 67°39'26'' W

VENEZUELA   Aguide

his youth when he wielded his sword under the orders of the Great Condé Louis of Bourbon—succeeded in driving the Dutch garrison from their slave-trading post of Gorée.

For the House of Orange, who had owned the island since 1588, this was a painful defeat. On December 6, d'Estrées landed his troops in Tobago. During the battle, the fort's gunpowder magazine exploded, killing the enemy staff and more than 250 soldiers.

> The admiral didn't want to listen to anyone. Neither questions about his tactics nor criticism of the skills of the captain he had chosen and whose qualities he continued to praise. If officers expressed their worry, he would merely respond with a shrug of the shoulders.

Sixteen Dutch ships struck their flag, and on December 29 they signed their capitulation. His victory was complete. But d'Estrées was still not satisfied. On May 7, 1678, he sailed from the Lesser Antilles to take the island of Curaçao, where privateers caused French merchant ships trouble, to occupy it "to such an extent that the Dutch will have no desire to return." With the help of the governor of Santo Domingo, the count shut himself away and carefully devised his plan. The admiral didn't want to listen to anyone. Neither questions about his tactics nor criticism of the skills of the captain he had chosen and whose qualities he continued to praise. If officers expressed their worry, he would merely respond with a shrug of the shoulders.

Consisting of seventeen men-of-war and privateer vessels, his fleet was one of the largest of the Sun King's regency. Confident as usual, he ordered to head for Orchila Island. But on the night of May 10 to 11, after three days of sailing, the small freebooter ships signaled with gunshots that they had run straight onto the reefs of the Las Aves archipelago, a blank spot on the maps of the time but well known by sailors as a place to be avoided. On deck of the

Terrible, his flagship, d'Estrées immediately ordered a turn, and a gust of wind let him begin the maneuver. However, just when the *Terrible* finally seemed in safety, her hull struck on a shoal and tore open with a deafening rattle.

Within a few minutes, the *Tonnant*, the *Prince*, the *Belliqueux*, the *Hercule*, the *Défenseur*, and the *Bourbon* each would strike on a shoal. His stubbornness had ruined the efforts of seven years of war. The island of Curaçao would remain Dutch.

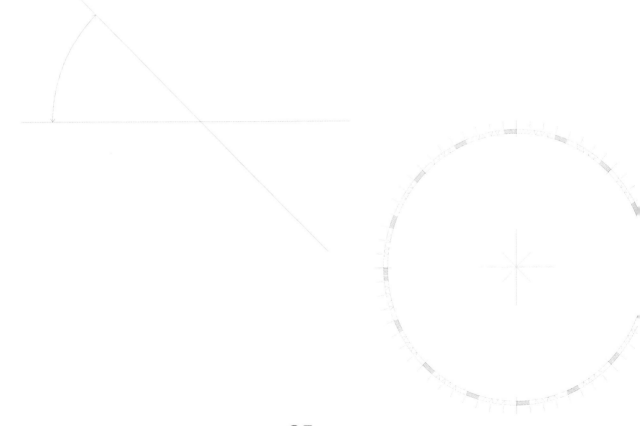

THE SILVER BENCH

HOW COMMANDER COUSTEAU EXPLORED THE WRECK OF A
FRENCH SHIP INSTEAD OF THAT OF A SPANISH GALLEON

24°00'04" N, 77°14'26" W

In July 1968, the crew of Commander Cousteau's famous *Calypso* returned from a long voyage to the Cape of Good Hope, passing by St. Helena, and was making its way to the Caribbean. The ship had to cast off on a new mission in South America, but Jacques Cousteau absolutely wanted to shoot images of an underwater excavation site and navigated in the vicinity of the Silver Bench, on the Santo Domingo coast, in search of the wreck of the Spanish galleon *Nuestra Señora de la Concepción*. In the days before she sank, on November 2, 1641, seven ships of the same convoy, caught in one of the worst hurricanes of the season, shipwrecked or crashed on the coast of Florida. Dismasted and in distress, what remained of the *Nuestra Señora de la Concepción* drifted slowly before encountering another storm and perishing on shoals. History repeated itself, and Madrid lost yet another considerable amount of gold and silver at the bottom of the sea.

Several search attempts were undertaken. But the ship had vanished, and the legend of its immense riches made the rounds in the Caribbean. In 1683, William Phips, an officer in the British navy born in a small town in Maine, managed to persuade the king to give him command of an eighteen-gun frigate, the HMS *Rose of Algiers*, to try to find the galleon. His first campaign failed, so he had to seek further royal consent before returning to the reefs with two ships, the *James and Mary* and the *Henry of London*. On January 29, 1687, the wreck was finally spotted and its cargo raised with the means they had on board. Upon his arrival at the English Downs, on Kent's east coast, on June 6, 1687, Phips brought back more than 34 tons of silver in "Spanish dollars,"

> Several search attempts were undertaken. But the ship had vanished, and the legend of its immense riches made the rounds in the Caribbean.

96

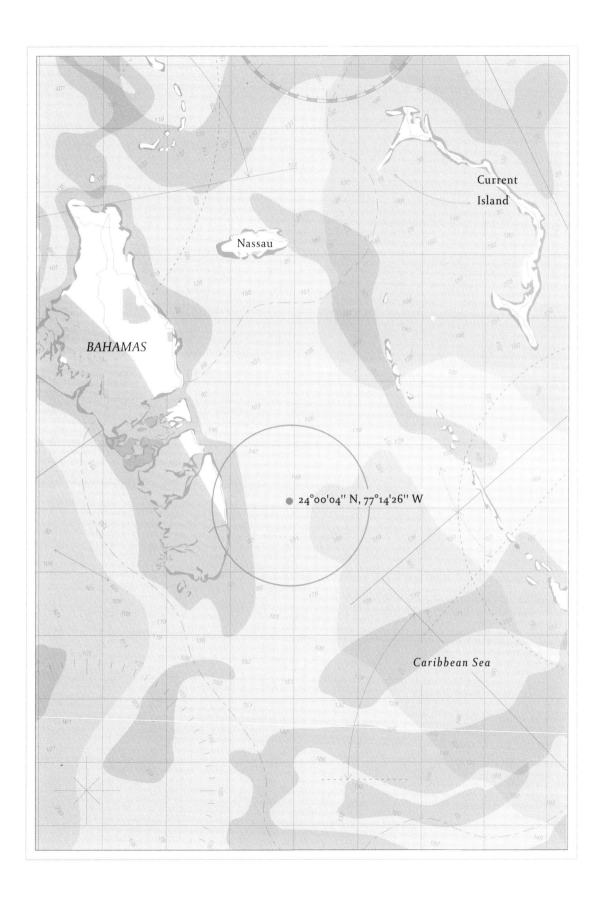

Current
Island

Nassau

BAHAMAS

● 24°00'04'' N, 77°14'26'' W

Caribbean Sea

ingots, and precious tableware, as well as dozens of pounds of gold and plenty of jewels.

An immense fortune. The officer received a share of the bounty and was knighted by James II. As the first royally appointed governor of the colony of Massachusetts, he was among those who eventually put an end to the collective hysteria that had

> On June 6, 1687, Phips brought back more than 34 tons of silver in "Spanish dollars," ingots, and precious tableware, as well as dozens of pounds of gold and plenty of jewels. An immense fortune.

taken hold of the Puritan community of Salem in 1692, where people suspected every woman to be a witch. But the failure of his military expeditions against the French in Acadia, New France, and Canada led to his being recalled to London,

where he died three years later virtually fallen into disgrace.

In 1968, convinced that William Phips had been able to raise only a small portion of the treasure of the *Nuestra Señora de la Concepción*, Rémy de Haenen, then mayor and general councilor of Saint-Barthélemy, Guadeloupe, decided to send Jacques-Yves Cousteau on another search mission. Very quickly, Bernard Delemotte, one of the crew members, retrieved a cannon and confirmed the discovery of an old wreck. But despite incessant dives and the careful inspection of more than 300 tons of coral debris, the exhausted men of the *Calypso* did not discover any treasures. Thanks to ceramic fragments and awls dating from 1756, they managed to identify the remains of an eighteenth-century French ship without being able to pinpoint exactly which.

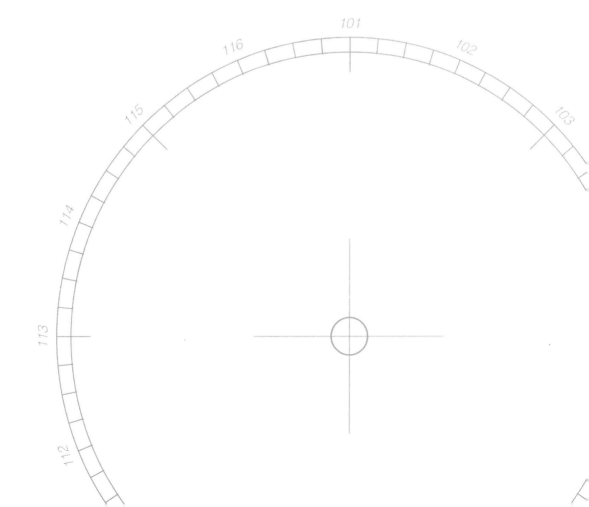

THE *BELEM*

BORN UNDER A LUCKY STAR

47°13'01" N, 01°33'28" W

Seafarers have always had a penchant for superstitions. In Douarnenez, for example, "rounded" figures (0, 2, 3, 5, 6, 8, and 9) were supposed to bring plentiful catches, while "straight" digits (1, 4, and 7) were dreaded to the extent that some skippers delayed their registration or ended up adding hook-shaped serifs to the font to ward off evil. And then there are those ships that, born under a lucky star, always seem to attract good fortune. Launched on June 10, 1896, the

> There are ships that, born under a lucky star, always seem to attract good fortune.

Belem is one of them. The only survivor of the great French commercial barques of the nineteenth century, she is not a clipper and has never circumnavigated Cape Horn or defied the storms of the southern oceans. She is a "West Indian," cut out to cross the Atlantic. The pride of the Nantes company Denis Crouan & Son, she was designed to transport cocoa on behalf of Menier chocolatiers and was named after the Brazilian city where the shipowners had founded a trading post. Despite her relatively modest dimensions—190 feet (58.5 meters) in length overall—her exceedingly elegant lines quickly earned her the nickname "yacht."

On May 7, 1902, when she arrived at the moorings of the port of Saint-Pierre, Martinique, she was refused entry due to a lack of space, so she had to anchor at Robert's Bay, at the other end of the island. The following day the port was engulfed in a *nuée ardente*—a cloud of hot gas and ash—as Mount Pelée erupted, burying the city of Saint-Pierre. More than thirty thousand people lost their lives and about fifteen ships sank in the bay, covered in a mixture of burning ash and mud. Miraculously sheltered, the *Belem* survived the disaster.

In 1914, while most of the large tall ships were rotting away in ship graveyards, the *Belem* was bought by the Duke of Westminster, who converted her into his private luxury pleasure yacht. Later sold to Irish

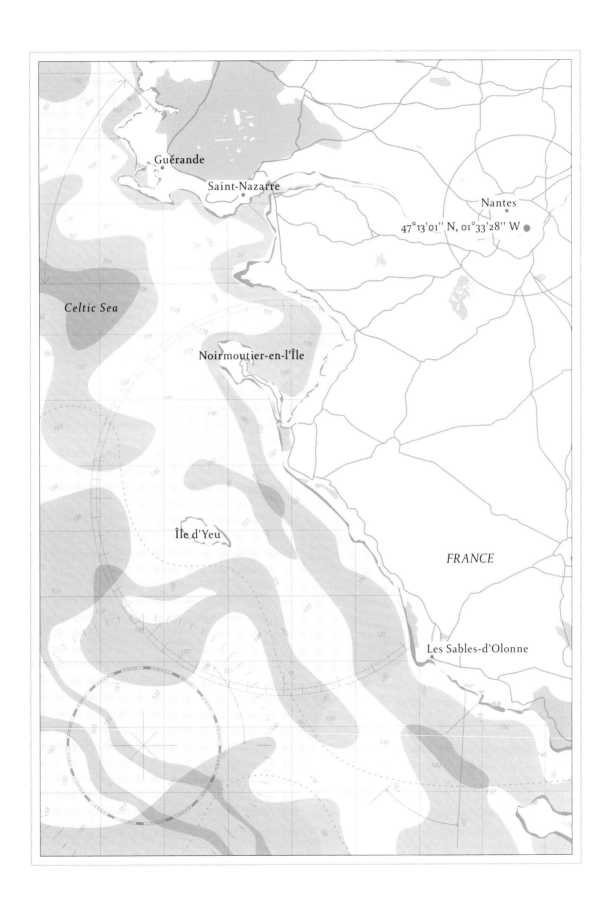

Guérande

Saint-Nazarre

Nantes

47°13'01'' N, 01°33'28'' W

Celtic Sea

Noirmoutier-en-l'Île

Île d'Yeu

FRANCE

Les Sables-d'Olonne

On a trip to Venice, Dr. Luc-Olivier Gosse recognized the old Nantes flagship and managed to excite other sailboat lovers for his cause. In 1984 she became one of the first ships to be classified as a historical monument. A year later, the *Belem* returned to sea and to Nantes, the city of her birth.

Giorgio Cini, her rigging was changed and she became a school ship of the Italian navy for the vocational training of orphans. Abandoned after 1965, she narrowly avoided being destroyed in a Venetian demolition site that tried to get rid of her. On a trip to Venice, Dr. Luc-Olivier Gosse, passionate about historical rigs, recognized the old Nantes flagship and managed to excite other sailboat lovers for his cause. On September 17, 1979, after lengthy negotiations, mainly between the Union Nationale des Caisses d'Épargne and the French public authorities, the *Belem* finally arrived in Brest, tugged by a French navy vessel. A foundation was set up with the far-fetched aim of putting her back in the water and turning her into a conservation site, passing on the tradition of the great sailing ships. In 1984 she became one of the first ships to be classified as a his-

brewer Arthur Ernest Guinness, she sailed around the world, renamed the *Fantôme II*. En route to Yokohama, Japan, around September 1, 1923, the crew lagged behind tacking into the headwinds and thus escaped a terrible earthquake ravaging the coast of the archipelago.

Even under a different flag, her luck never ran out. On the eve of World War II, she was moored on the Isle of Wight to be laid up. Spared German bombing, she briefly served as a base for a unit of the Free French Naval Forces; then, renamed the

torical monument. A year later, the *Belem* returned to sea and to Nantes, the city of her birth. Her new life has only just begun.

THE *MARY CELESTE*

HOW THE MOST FAMOUS GHOST SHIP OF HER TIME
ENDED UP STRANDED ON A ROCK

18°58'16" N, 72°17'06" W

On December 4, 1872, in the Atlantic Ocean, off the Azores, the *Mary Celeste* entered the dark annals of ocean lore. On that day, the helmsman of the *Dei Gratia*, a commercial sailboat en route to Gibraltar, saw a ship advancing as if she was in distress. Most of her brails were haled up, while other sails were flapping freely or seemed torn off. Ignoring all signals, one of his comrades, and the two men had seen each other recently, just before they had gone off to sea. At thirty-seven, Briggs was a respected sailor, and his family had a good reputation in New England, where he was born. He had left New York a month earlier with nine people in tow: his wife, Sarah; his two-year-old daughter, Sophia Mathilda; and seven sailors. He was to deliver 1,700 barrels of denatured alcohol to the port of Genoa, Italy. Meticulous and a devout believer, he had chosen his officers carefully and recruited confident and experienced sailors.

The lifeboat was missing from the deck, and the crew had vanished. There was no one left. What had happened? The last entry in the logbook was dated November 25, 8:00 a.m.

The lifeboat was missing from the deck, and the crew had vanished. There was no one left. What had happened? The last entry in the logbook was dated November 25, 8:00 a.m.—that is, nine days earlier—and stated that the *Mary Celeste* was cruising about 750 miles southwest of its current position.

The cargo in the hold was intact, and the abundant provisions were neatly stored.

the vessel continued its zigzagging course for about 10 nautical miles. Intrigued, the ship's captain, David Morehouse, decided to approach to come to her aid. But when he recognized the shape of the American brigantine *Mary Celeste*, his heart sank. Benjamin Briggs, her captain, was

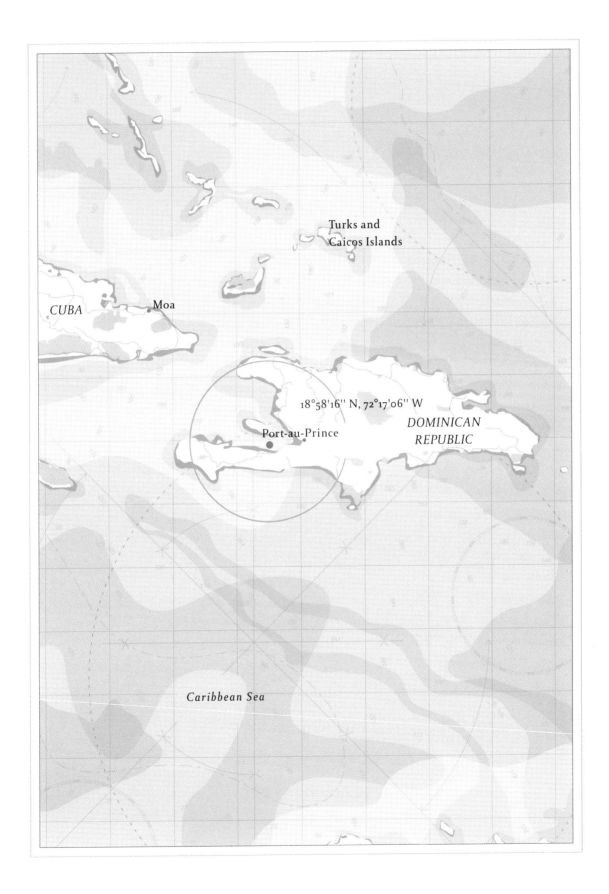

CUBA

Moa

Turks and
Caicos Islands

18°58'16" N, 72°17'06" W

DOMINICAN
REPUBLIC

Port-au-Prince

Caribbean Sea

Briggs's cabin was pretty orderly, as were those of the sailors and the chief mate, but the navigational instruments were nowhere to be found. In the storeroom, everything was in its place, and the stoves in the galley were clean. The captain of the *Dei Gratia*, who decided to take the *Mary Celeste* with him to Gibraltar, could not find any signs of a hasty departure or confrontation. On December 13 the two ships were in dock, and the abandoned ship was sealed off by the Maritime Court. Upon examining the sailboat, the inspectors found reddish drips and notches on the bow and ship's rail, resembling those left by an ax or sword. The attorney general of Gibraltar, Frederick Solly-Flood, charged with investigating the case, is convinced that a crime has taken place. He concludes that the sailors, under the influence of alcohol, mur-dered the Briggs family before leaving the ship on the lifeboat. But his theory does not hold up. Further analysis quickly rules out the presence of blood and shows that the marks were caused by the action of the swell on the timber. On February 25 the prosecutor has to release the ship, which returns to sea with a new crew. In the ports, tongues were loose and people were convinced that Captain Morehouse had murdered Benjamin Briggs and his family with his own hands, or that the two men had agreed to share the reward offered by the insurance company before making off to South America. Some alleged an act of piracy but were unable to explain why the ship and its cargo had remained untouched. According to another theory, a waterspout might have suddenly formed, destroying the rigging and giving the instant impression of a shipwreck. In the press, alleged survivors or former sailors made up stories, and journalists even wondered if the brigantine had perhaps been attacked by a kraken.

> The captain of the *Dei Gratia*, who decided to take the *Mary Celeste* with him to Gibraltar, could not find any signs of a hasty departure or confrontation.

Toxic and a source of fear, the *Mary Celeste* continued to sail, but her various owners struggled to recruit a crew.

Every possible theory was considered, from the Bermuda Triangle to Atlantis and aliens. Even Arthur Conan Doyle, the inventor of Sherlock Holmes, gave his version of events. But the enigma remains unresolved.

Toxic and a source of fear, the *Mary Celeste* continued to sail, but her various owners struggled to recruit a crew. In 1885, determined to get rid of a cursed ship, the last shipowners loaded her with worthless cargo and arranged her sinking on a coral reef between the main island of Haiti and Gonâve Island. At sea, fear is a poison.

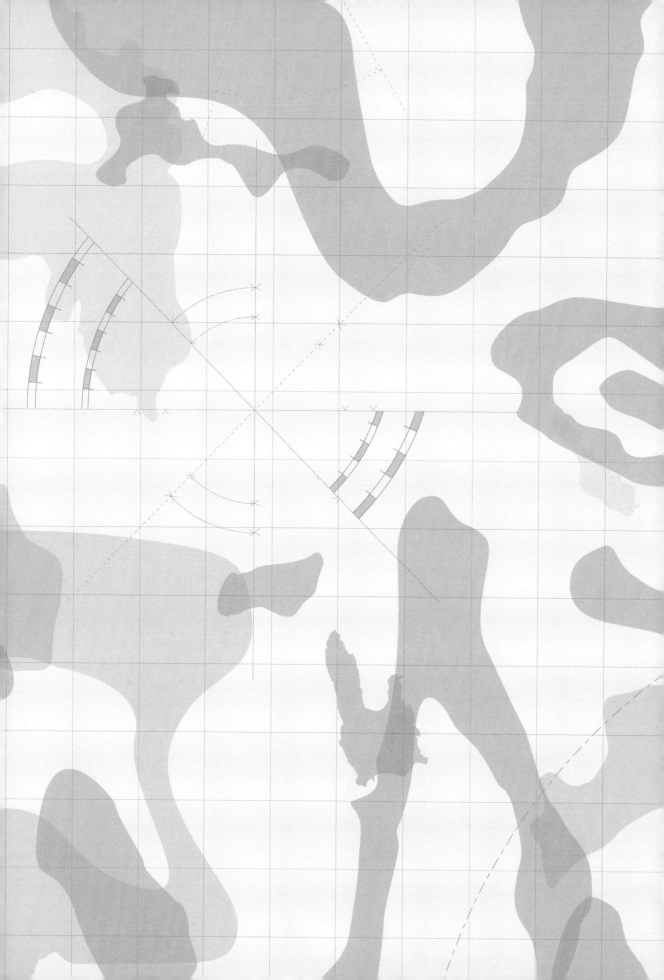

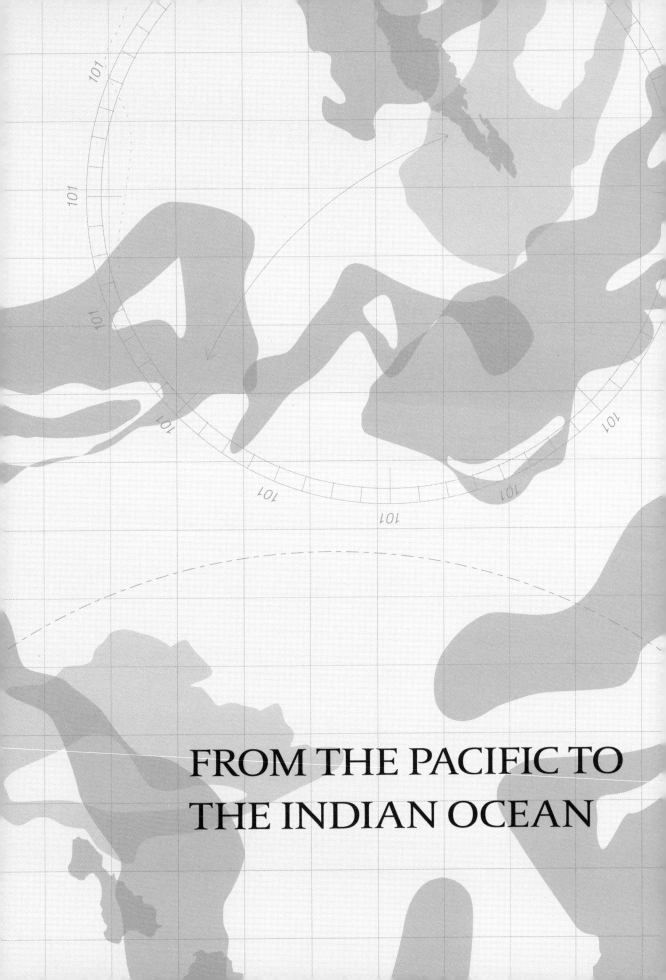

FROM THE PACIFIC TO
THE INDIAN OCEAN

THE CLIPPER *TAMARIS*, PIG ISLAND, AND THIRTEEN CASTAWAYS . . .

AND THE ALBATROSS THAT, QUITE INVOLUNTARILY, TRIED TO RESCUE THEM

46°06' S, 50°14' E

On December 3, 1886, without much fanfare, the clipper *Tamaris*, owned by Bordes merchant shipowners, sailed from Bordeaux, France, for Nouméa, New Caledonia. On board, the crew of twelve men at the orders of Captain Jean-Pierre Majou mechanically carried out their maneuvers.

> But come August, there had not been any more news of the *Tamaris*, and Lloyd, her insurance company, reported her loss. Like others before her, the sailing vessel had undoubtedly sunk with all hands.

The journey was going to be long, but the men were used to it. If they did not encounter any problems, they should reach New Caledonia around March 15, 1887,

and return to France via Cape Horn in June. But come August, there had not been any more news of the *Tamaris*, and Lloyd, her insurance company, reported her loss. Like others before her, the sailing vessel had undoubtedly sunk with all hands, and the families of the sailors began to mourn.

The story could end here, but everything changed on September 25, 1887. That morning, on a beach in Western Australia, near Fremantle, walkers noticed an exhausted albatross lying in the sand. On land, encounters with these great overseas travelers are so rare that the bird's presence intrigued them. But what they discovered as they approached it amazed them even more: the bird was wearing a sheet-metal plate around its neck, engraved with the French words "13 shipwrecked men fled to the Crozet Islands. Help, for the love of God! August 11, 1887." The Australian authorities immediately notified the French consul, and on November 18 the French navy aviso *Meurthe*, based in Madagascar and under the command of Lieutenant Frédéric Richard-Foy, sailed

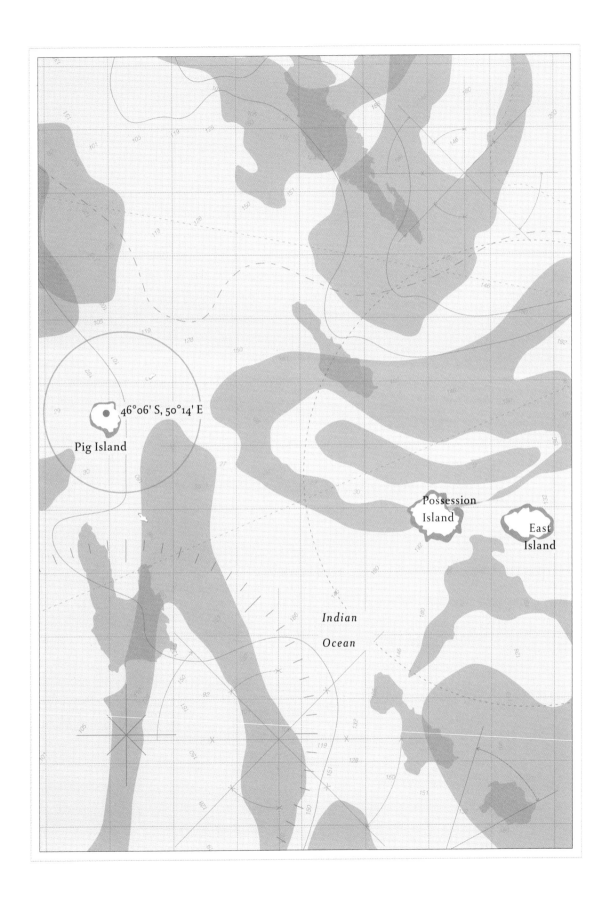

46°06' S, 50°14' E

Pig Island

Possession
Island

East
Island

Indian

Ocean

from Sainte-Marie, Réunion, to search the archipelago. The albatross messenger had taken more than six weeks to travel 3,000 miles, and there was no evidence that the crew of the *Tamaris* was still alive. The weather conditions at sea were particularly difficult, and the aviso had to wait until December 1 to be able to send out a raft. In a shelter they discovered on Pig Island, the soldiers found Majou's logbook,

But the days are long, the hope of being rescued is dwindling, and food is starting to run out. Morale is at a low. The captain tries to convince his men to set out for the largest island of the archipelago, Possession Island.

in which he announced his departure to the neighboring Possession Island on September 30. With no time to waste, the aviso immediately set off for the island.

But the crew did not find anyone. Neither there nor on East Island, nor even on the Îlots des Apôtres, north of Pig Island, and Richard-Foy eventually gave up the search on December 16, convinced that the boat with the survivors had drifted south and been swallowed by the sea.

From what we know today, three and a half months after leaving Bordeaux, the *Tamaris* got into difficulties in the vicinity of Tristan da Cunha, north of the Roaring Forties, and faced increasingly high waves. On the night of March 8 to 9, 1887, the sailboat struck a reef southwest of Penguin Island, in the Crozet archipelago, and sank within a few hours. The crew, who managed to launch a rowing boat and take provisions and tools with them, decided to make for Pig Island. The area was uninhabited, but Majou knew that eight years earlier the *Comus*, an English vessel, had left a shelter behind with food, clothing, and equipment

112

for seal hunting. On March 11 they landed and got their hands on what they were hoping for. After a few weeks, they started to swap the sea biscuit, dried meat, and fish they had found for seal meat and penguin eggs.

To warm up, they would light a peat fire. But the days are long, the hope of being rescued is dwindling, and food is starting to run out. Morale is at a low. The captain tries to convince his men to set out for the largest land of the archipelago, Possession Island, about 50 miles in the direction of the prevailing winds, where more ships pass. But they are not ready yet. Jean-Yves Le Guen, a novice on board, who has just turned eighteen and is desperately bored, comes up with the idea of catching albatrosses and attaching metal plates to their necks with a Mayday message. You never know; they have nothing to lose. On September 30, five days after one of the birds lands in Australia and two months before the arrival of rescue, the survivors of the *Tamaris* decide to go off to sea. No one would ever see them again, but the reefs south of Penguin Island now bear the name

"brisant to Tamaris" (Tamaris Shoal), Pig Island has its "Meurthe Moorings," and the volcano, the highest point of the island, was named "Mont Richard-Foy."

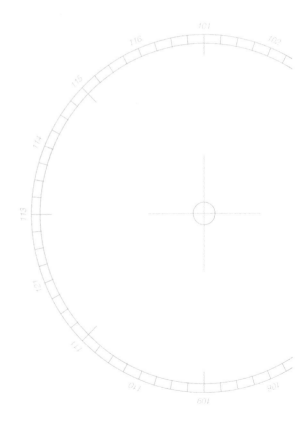

CAPTAIN KIDD'S FABULOUS TREASURE

HOW TO TURN LEAD INTO MONEY

16°50' S, 49°55' E

For three long weeks, swinging in the wind, the tortured body of Captain Kidd, one of the most famous pirates of his time, remained hanging on the banks of the Thames. In this pleasant month of May 1701, England no longer tolerated these self-made gentlemen who still roamed the

> The former Scottish merchant turned privateer, then pirate, made the mistake of targeting an English ship.

seas without respecting the flag of His Gracious Majesty, and his sinister silhouette, covered with tar, remained there to warn those who had not gotten the message yet. If Captain Kidd had been content with haranguing the French or sinking the Spanish or the Dutch, he might have escaped the noose. But the former Scottish merchant turned privateer, then pirate, had made the mistake of targeting

an English ship. And the influential lords who had shares in the *Adventure Galley*, his thirty-four-gun sailboat, dropped him. Hardly anyone was sorry about his death, and the story of his fabulous fortune, hidden somewhere in Madagascar, was still open ended.

Opportunities for pirates became few and far between. In the Caribbean, Spanish galleons loaded with gold and silver were becoming increasingly rare. On Tortuga Island—French since 1697—the Brethren of the Coast were no longer welcome, and most of the taverns and brothels in Jamaica—a feature that had earned Port Royal a reputation in the days of Sir Henry Morgan—were swallowed up by the great earthquake of June 7, 1692. The last remaining European pirates were now confined to the bay of Ambodifotatra in the waters of Madagascar, around Sainte-Marie Island, at the crossroads of the major trade routes between the Red Sea and the Indian Ocean. Like Captain Kidd, Henry Avery—alias "Long Ben"—the frightful Thomas Tew, Olivier Levasseur—nicknamed "the Buzzard"—or Christopher Condent—better known as "Billy One-

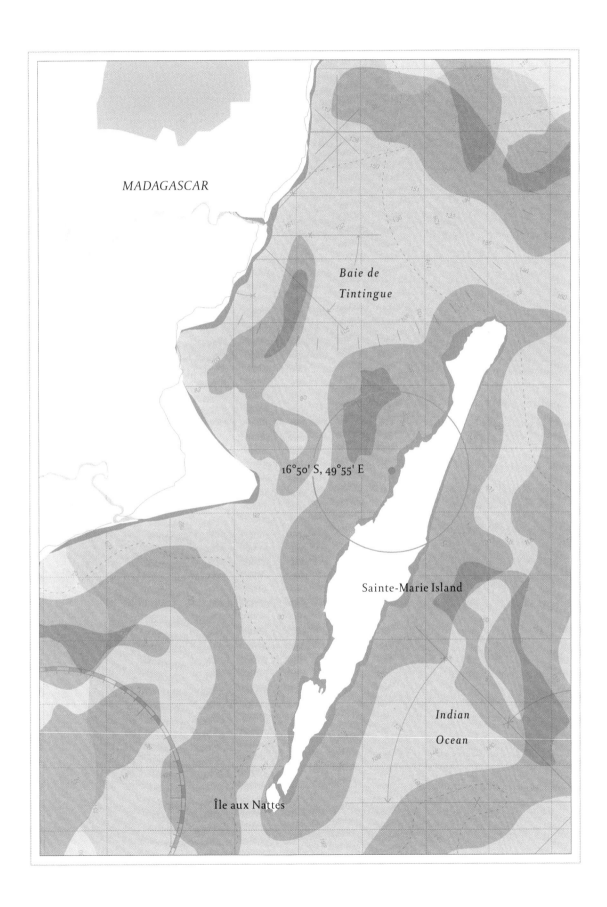

MADAGASCAR

Baie de
Tintingue

16°50' S, 49°55' E

Sainte-Marie Island

Indian

Ocean

Île aux Nattes

With their black flag hoisted to the mainmast, an eye patch, and a parrot on one shoulder, they drink rum while kissing women and roam the seas of the world aboard proud crafts. Almost everything about this is wrong, of course, but the legend has developed a life of its own, and with it come fabulous stories of hidden treasures.

developed a life of its own, and with it come fabulous stories of hidden treasures: more gold than one person could ever spend, jewels worthy of the greatest sovereigns, and tons of silver ingots—such as the one lifted from the muddy seabed of the bay of the Îlot Madame, on Sainte-Marie Island, in May 2015 by one of the most famous American underwater explorers. That day, in front of cameras from around the world, adventurer Barry Clifford and his team exhibited a gray bar weighing more than 99 pounds (45 ki-

hand"—liked to drop anchor there. But even here, their days were numbered.

In the nineteenth century, literature turned them into romantic and cruel heroes. With their black flag hoisted to the mainmast, an eye patch, and a parrot on one shoulder, they drink rum while kissing women and roam the seas of the world aboard proud crafts. Almost everything about this is wrong, of course, but the legend has

los) found in a wreck that could well have been that of the famous Scottish pirate's ship. Their discovery was exceptional. Embossed with marks and stamps, the ingot looked like silver. But the object handed over with great pomp to Madagascar's resident Hery Rajaonarimampianina, who had come to witness the event with members of his government and the ambassadors of the United States and Great Britain, quickly

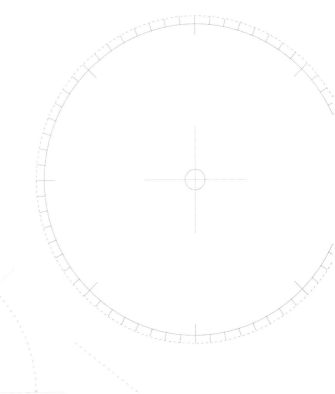

turned out to contain 95 percent lead. But it got worse:

Worried about the possible risks of looting Malagasy heritage, UNESCO sent its own experts to the site, who concluded without appeal that "what was announced as the wreck of pirate Captain Kidd's *Adventure Galley* is probably part of old port structures." The American's dream turned into a nightmare. His only consolation was that, according to the international organization, "several historical wrecks" that would be of "considerable archaeological interest" were located nearby. Nothing was lost, save honor.

CHITTAGONG AND ALANG, WHERE GIANTS COME TO DIE

A MARITIME LANDFILL SITE

22°20'51" N, 91°48'44" E

While English invariably uses "she" to refer to a clipper, a ferry, or a warship, French prefers the male pronoun "he" in these cases. A usage that speaks volumes, perhaps, about the nature of the relationship that two nations have forged with the maritime world. But in Chittagong Bay, Bangladesh, or on the coast of Alang, India, the subject of gender no longer matters. When a ship gets stranded there, it is on its deathbed. Here, like hundreds of others before her, the ocean liner *France*, which became the *Blue Lady*, ended up in spare parts sold on the Indian market. In the Bangladeshi port of Chittagong, transformed into a maritime landfill site, an army of scrap metal dealers take apart discarded supertankers, old-fashioned cruise ships, or large ore carriers past their use-by date—with their bare hands. Huge cut-open freighters are rusting away everywhere on the oil-drenched sand as far as the eye can see. With government approval, shipowners and petroleum companies from all over the world come here to get rid of their old vessels. Since 1960, these organized shipwrecks have met part of the country's steel demand. And in slums, the arrival of a new hull to be dismantled is a godsend. It provides a guarantee of work, of earning a little money and not going hungry for a few weeks—so people fight over who gets to slave away in the mud. One hundred thousand people live more or less off this activity, and a large percentage of the Bangladeshi metal industry works with remnants from Chittagong. The procedure is always the same: At high tide, the condemned ship glides in on the silt; then, as soon as the tide recedes, the scrap metal workers come to tow it, before tackling what remains of its enormous structure. Armed with shovels, pickaxes, hammers, and blow torches, the workers labor day and night. Everything is methodically dismantled, starting with the tanks, siphoned to the last drop. Then they turn to the furniture: lamps, tables, vats, dishes, etc., which end up at local markets. After that it's time to deal with the more serious stuff: salvaging the hull, which is cut by the square foot with blow torches and dragged to the docks by using winches and hundreds of arms. At this rate it takes only two months to reduce a supertanker to a pile of blackened girders. But this manna of iron and sheet metal comes at a price: fatal accidents are legion, and pollution has reached unprecedented levels. None of this matters, however, because here, more than anywhere else, necessity dictates the rules.

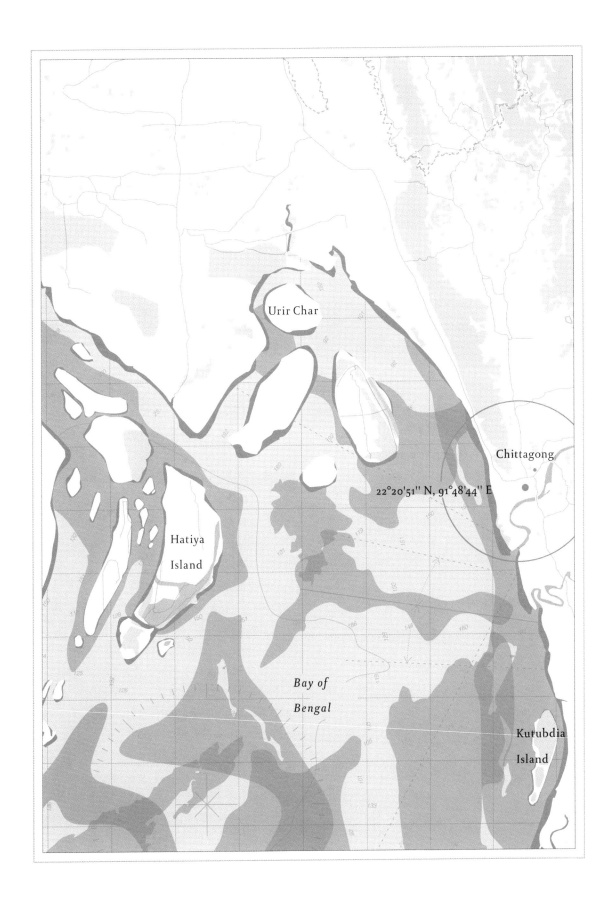

Urir Char

Chittagong

22°20'51" N, 91°48'44" E

Hatiya
Island

Bay of
Bengal

Kutubdia
Island

THE SCHOONER
GRAFTON

WHAT INSPIRED JULES VERNE TO WRITE *THE MYSTERIOUS ISLAND*

————— ◊ —————

50°42' S, 166°05' E

In Nantes, one fine day in summer 1839, a young Jules Verne escaped the watchful eyes of his parents and tried to sign on aboard the three-master *Coralie* as a cabin boy, leaving for India. At eleven years of age, the child who dreamed of islands, exotic ports, and great voyages wanted to travel the seas to gift a coral necklace to his cousin Caroline. He made it along the Loire before being narrowly caught in Paimboeuf by his father—and back onshore, severe punishment awaited him. But that day would mark his life, and the world of seafaring would never leave him. In 1868, on board his first boat, the *Saint Michel*,

a rowboat designed for hobby fishing, he sailed in the Somme Bay and tacked off the coast of Le Crotoy, France. Having become a member of the Yacht Club of France and garnered some success, Jules Verne had the *Saint Michel II* built in 1876, a luxurious "swallow of the English Channel" of 43 feet (13 meters), which he replaced a few months later with the *Saint Michel III*, a 102-foot-long (31 meter) steam yacht equipped with a crew of nine men with whom he traveled the Mediterranean, the Atlantic, and the North Sea all the way to the Baltic Sea. When planning a sequel to *Twenty Thousand Leagues under the Sea* and *Voyages extraordinaires*, he wrote the odyssey of a shipwrecked family abandoned on a desert island: *Shipwrecked Family: Marooned with Uncle Robinson*. But his publisher, Pierre-Jules Hetzel, did not share his enthusiasm and refused to publish it.

One story would haunt him forever. Like many of his contemporaries, Jules Verne had read, in the magazine *Le Tour du Monde*, the account of the wreck of the schooner *Grafton* in the Auckland Islands, whose crew had remained captive on a reef for twenty months. One detail particularly

> When planning a sequel to *Twenty Thousand Leagues under the Sea* and *Voyages extraordinaires*, he wrote the odyssey of a shipwrecked family abandoned on a desert island: *Shipwrecked Family: Marooned with Uncle Robinson*.

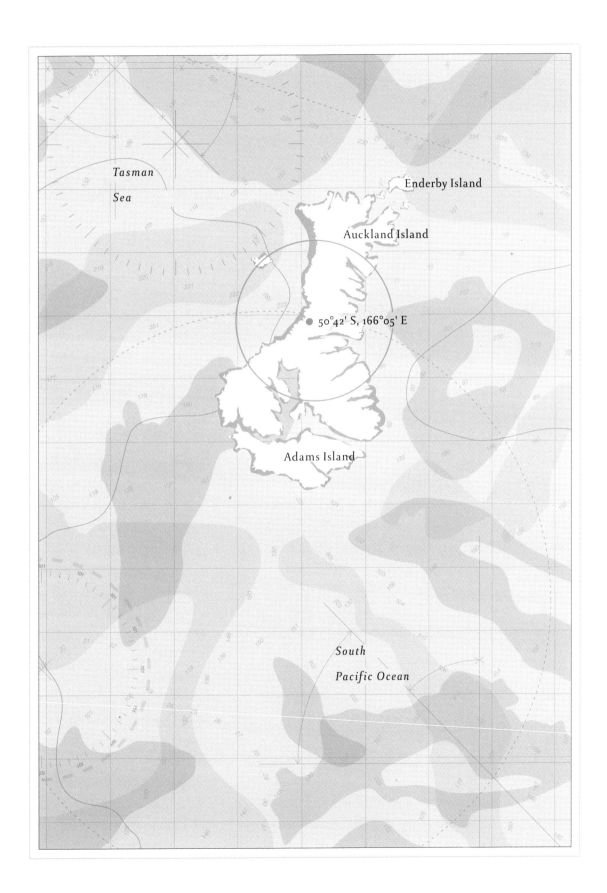

Tasman
Sea

Enderby Island

Auckland Island

● 50°42' S, 166°05' E

Adams Island

South

Pacific Ocean

intrigued him: among the five survivors of the disaster, a Frenchman—the narrator François Édouard Raynal—seemed like the perfect character for a novel. Born on July 8, 1830, in Moissac, France, the son of a bankrupt bourgeois family had signed on as a cabin boy on a three-master at the age of fourteen . . .

Jules Verne was captivated. At nineteen, the young adventurer is already the manager of a sugar cane plantation in Mauritius, which he leaves to seek his fortune in Australia, where he hopes to find local gold. Sick with cholera, he miraculously survives

ney, on November 12, 1863, and becomes part of a small group of pioneers who hope to reach Campbell Island to exploit its silver mines. But the men find nothing but wind and dust and decide to sail to the Auckland Islands, about 289 miles (465 kilometers) south of New Zealand, where there is said to be an abundance of gold. On December 31, 1863, they enter the strait north of Adams Island to drop anchor and seek shelter from stormy weather. On January 3, driven by increasingly violent gales in the sea of Carnley Harbour, the schooner's anchor breaks off and the ship drives straight into the rocks. Four sailors—American captain Thomas Musgrave, Norwegian Alexander McLaren, Englishman George Harris, Portuguese cook Henri Forgé—and Raynal manage to reach dry land. Covered with thick vegetation, the islet is uninhabited but lies on the main route for whalers hunting cetaceans in the South Pacific. While waiting for help, the survivors get organized and swear on Captain Musgrave's Bible to support each

> While waiting for help, the survivors get organized and swear on Captain Musgrave's Bible to support each other, come what may. Raynal distinguishes himself with his ingenuity.

but contracts an inflammation that leaves him blind for ten days. Raynal boards the *Grafton*, an 80-ton schooner based in Syd-

other, come what may. Very quickly Raynal distinguishes himself with his ingenuity.

Using the shells and sand found on the shore, he invents a kind of cement that allows them to add a fireplace to the cabin they built with branches and timber recovered from the schooner. Armed with a rifle, an ax, and a hammer, they hunt birds and sea lions, whose skins they tan to make clothes and shoes. By mixing wrack collected from the shore with oil, the Frenchman makes soap . . . and when they struggle to catch seals, they eat mussels and fish. A few months after their arrival, the *Invercauld*, a Scottish three-master, shipwrecks on the other side of the island, on the reefs of the northwestern tip. But the survivors, rescued a year later by a passing brig, never meet those of the *Grafton*.

Despite the bad weather, the cold, the rain, and the flies that harass them, their spirits are high. But the five men realize the obvious: help will not come. It's been too long since they disappeared, and nobody is looking for them. Using a makeshift forge, the sailors fashion tools and nails to transform their rowing boat into a closed-deck boat, able to withstand the sea. After seven months of hard work, the dinghy rigged with canvas recovered from the *Grafton* and baptized *Rescousse* is completed. But she can fit only three people. Harris and Forgés will remain on the island. Musgrave, Raynal, and McLaren swear to return for them and leave the island on July 19, 1865. After five days and five nights of difficult sailing in one of the most dangerous seas in the world, the three men reach Port Adventure on Stewart Island, 300 nautical miles farther north.

Two days later they set sail again aboard a small sailboat, the cutter *Flying Scud*, to keep their promise and pick up their two companions. But they're faced with ferocious winds, and the round trip takes seven weeks. After he recovered, Raynal wrote his memoirs and sailed for a few more years in the South Seas. He became a tax official on his return to France and spent the last years of his life in Valence-d'Agen, in the Tarn-et-Garonne region of France, where he died April 28, 1898. He never met Jules Verne, who was nevertheless largely inspired by his account to write *The Mysterious Island*, his famous novel that Hetzel published without hesitation in 1874.

THE TREASURE OF THE *SAN DIEGO*

THE END OF THE MANILA GALLEON

14°31' N, 120°46' E

Thanks to the first explorations carried out by the conquistadors beyond the isthmus of Panama in 1513, and to Magellan's trip to the Philippines between 1520 and 1521, the Pacific became Spanish. In the sixteenth century the Spanish Crown had the undivided power over this immense sea that led to Asia and its riches. But its domination was threatened. By Portugal, first of all, which contested Japan. Then by the Dutch and their powerful East India Company. But Spain had a stronghold in Manila. Since Andrés de Urdaneta's first voyage in

> ## Heavy and poorly defended in the open sea, the galleons also attracted English privateers and pirates of the likes of Francis Drake.

1565, the sea route between Mexico and the Philippines had been the reserve of the Spanish. At the time, four galleons loaded with Chinese goods, fabrics, precious met-

als, and spices provided the link between the two continents each year. But the king eventually allowed only two ships, then only one, to make the crossing. On the other side of the ocean, in Acapulco, life was dictated by the rhythm of the great fair that opened its doors when these galleons arrived. After months of boredom, the dab colonial city finally emerged from its torpor, and the streets were teeming with people. Then the galleons left again, filled to the brim with silver pried from Mexican soil. Dictated by the southwestern monsoon, all ships had to leave Manila in June, because starting in July, powerful headwinds picked up. As soon as they had left the archipelago behind, the boats headed northeast, passing north of the Mariana Islands, and set their sails for the ocean between the 31st and 44th degrees north latitude. An uncertain, dangerous, and seemingly endless crossing aboard overloaded ships, which could last up to eight months. Between 1580 and 1630, sea fortunes were legion, and more than half of Manila's galleons disappeared with all hands. Heavy and poorly defended in the open sea, the galleons also attracted English privateers and

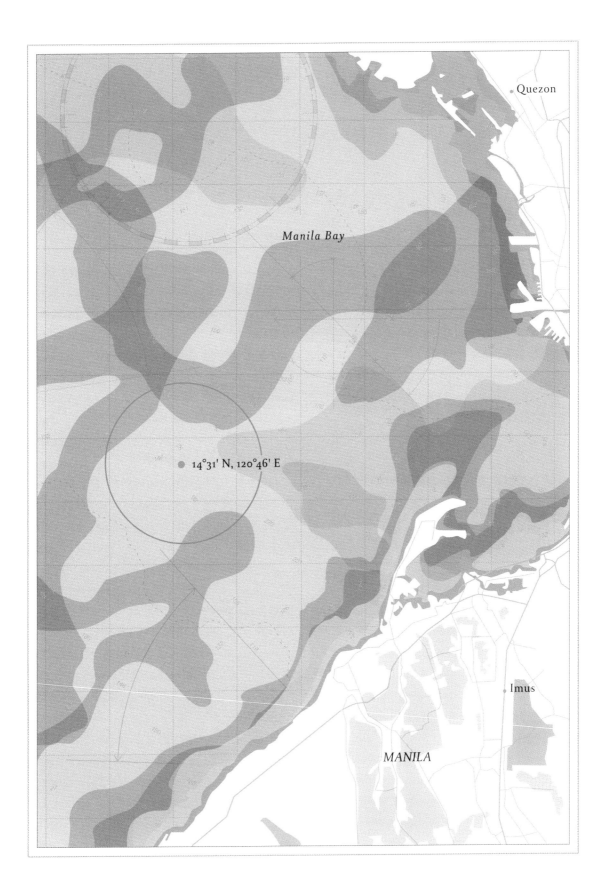

Quezon

Manila Bay

14°31' N, 120°46' E

Imus

MANILA

pirates of the likes of Francis Drake, whose arrival in the Southeast Pacific between 1579 and 1580 changed the story forever. About fifteen years later, the Dutch, in turn, entered the race, and the provocations multiplied. On July 2, 1598, Olivier Van Noort, a privateer from Utrecht, left Rotterdam with four ships and the firm intention of attack-

> On July 2, 1598, Olivier Van Noort left Rotterdam with four ships and the firm intention of attacking Spanish and Portuguese possessions in the Pacific.

ing Spanish and Portuguese possessions in the Pacific. After a difficult Atlantic crossing, he reached Rio de Janeiro, where he was bombarded, then coasted along Brazil and Argentina, torching everything he could along the way. After crossing the Strait of Magellan, his vessels split up and went back up the coast. But Don Luis de Velasco y Castilla, the viceroy of New Spain, sent out his ships and waited for Van Noort at the coast of Peru. The latter decided not to sail north and thus escaped the trap, in-

stead heading for the Islas de los Ladrones before entering the Bay of the Philippines in October 1600. Manila was in shock, and Governor Francisco de Tello de Guzmán was taken short. His city was unarmed, and the arsenal had no warship capable of fighting off the invader. After lengthy hesitation, Tello instructed Antonio de Morga, his lieutenant governor and high-court official, to assemble a fleet as quickly as possible. Within thirty days, two galleys, a 50-ton patache, the *San Bartolomé*, and the *San Diego*—a 300-ton merchant galleon armed with fourteen guns—were ready to defend the colony. On December 11, Antonio de Morga—who had been appointed commander of the fleet despite his complete inexperience in naval combat—proudly watched the crews board, accompanied by soldiers, hidalgos—the top of the crops of Manila—and Japanese mercenaries. More than 450 people crammed onto the *San Diego*, whose holds were already full of goods. The morning of December 12, the galleon and the patache weighed their anchors, eager to sink the Dutch fleet. On December 14 they were within sight of the *Mauritius* and the *Eendracht*, Olivier Van Noort's two ships. The *San Diego* had hoisted all her sails and immediately rushed toward the *Mauritius*, which fired a devastating first broadside onto her rigging. But the galleon was so heavy and its decks so crowded that it was unable to retort the attack. Morga was furious. In a fit of anger, he decided to charge at the enemy and strike him at full speed. Due to the impact, the two boats wavered and the three hundred men-at-arms of the *San Diego* quickly outmaneuvered the Dutch. In the confusion, and despite the orders she was given, the *San Bartolomé* retreated from the battle and tried to catch

The galleon was so heavy and its decks so crowded that it was unable to retort the attack.

up with the *Eendracht*, which had made off. A fire broke out, giving some of the sailors of the *Mauritius* the chance to pick up their arms again. Then the *San Diego*, which had suffered a blow under the waterline, began to sink dangerously low. Antonio de Morga panicked and cut off the moorings and tethers that prevented her from maneuvering. Freed from her opponent, she slowly drifted to the small island of Fortuna, where she hoped to strand. But her main masts were broken, and because there was but a single sail left on the bowsprit, she had become unmaneuverable. Within minutes, while the *Mauritius*, unexpectedly victorious, returned to the open sea, the *San Diego* sank from the front, and she sank quickly, taking almost all of her crew with her. Holding tightly on to a mattress, Morga survived the disaster and tried to save his head by blaming his chief mate for the sinking. Manila had been saved—but at what price?

Discovered in April 1991 by underwater archeologist Franck Goddio, the wreck of the *San Diego* is resting at 170 feet deep (52 meters) 0.7 miles (1.2 kilometers) from Fortuna. Her treasures, including rare coins, magnificent gold jewelry, countless pieces of porcelain from the Ming dynasty, weapons, and cannons, have traveled around the world. As has the sorry story of Antonio de Morga, the magistrate who, in a battle, believed himself to be a sailor.

LAPÉROUSE'S FINAL MYSTERY

IN SEARCH OF THE *BOUSSOLE* AND THE *ASTROLABE*

11°39' S, 166°54' E

Departing from Brest on August 1, 1785, the *Boussole* and the *Astrolabe* headed off to the Pacific as part of what was to be the largest expedition of the late eighteenth century. As is often the case, the two scows, kitted out as frigates, were a little on the heavy side up at the front and tricky to maneuver. In Madeira, where they made a first stop for repairs, the scientists on board and some passengers who had not yet earned their sea legs and were overcome by seasickness took a breather. Louis XVI himself had commis-

> Louis XVI himself had commissioned their journey and had set very ambitious goals for Jean-François de Galaup, Comte de Lapérouse.

sioned their journey and had set very ambitious goals for Jean-François de Galaup, Comte de Lapérouse, a brilliant captain, scholar, and sophisticated gentleman to whom he had entrusted this enterprise. After having recovered its settlements in India and part of its colonies in Canada thanks to the Treaty of Paris (1783), France considered itself a world power yet again, and the king wanted to complete the mapping of the globe, open new maritime and trade routes, establish new colonial trading posts, and expand scientific knowledge while fighting against the influence of its archrival, England. Since the death of English explorer James Cook, killed in the Sandwich Islands, Hawaii, six years earlier, the field was yet again open in the Pacific, and Versailles dreamed of a new Louis Antoine de Bougainville. Invited to "describe without prejudice and to compile a critical catalog of knowledge in all areas of knowledge," Lapérouse, who was about to celebrate his forty-fourth birthday, was given carte blanche. On August 13 the two ships arrived in Tenerife. Seriously ill, astronomer Louis Monge left the ship. Alongside naturalist Jean-Nicolas Dufresne, who disembarked at Macau on February 1, 1787, the naval guard Henri Mel de Saint-Céran, who was let go in Manila two months later, and the diplomat

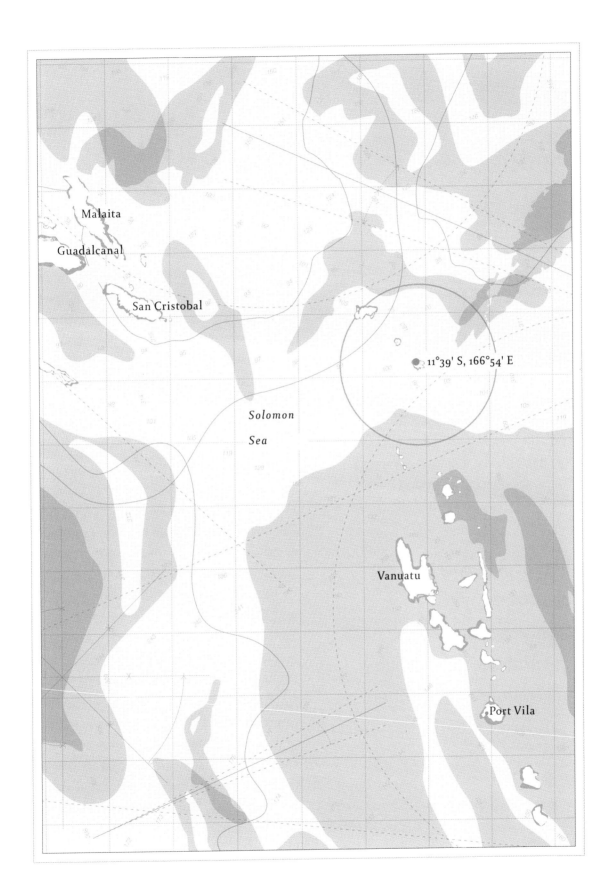

Malaita

Guadalcanal

San Cristobal

Solomon

Sea

11°39' S, 166°54' E

Vanuatu

Port Vila

Barthélemy de Lesseps, who was left in Petropavlovsk, Kamchatka, in September with some of the expedition's records, Monge would be one of the few to return alive. Because from March 10, 1788, there was no further news of the crew.

In his last letter sent from Botany Bay, Australia, Lapérouse seems enthusiastic and announces his imminent departure for the Friendly Islands, the present-day Tonga archipelago. "I shall," he writes, "examine every thing that falls in my way;

> But the *Astrolabe* and the *Boussole* disappeared. Despite several search expeditions, the 219 men of Lapérouse's expedition were never found.

. . . the southwest coast of New Caledonia, the island of Santa-Cruz de Mendaña, the southern coast of the land of the Ar-

sacides, with that of Louisiada, as far as New Guinea; and in this part I shall seek another channel than Endeavour Strait. The months of August, September, and part of October, I shall employ in visiting the Gulf of Carpentaria, and the west coast of New Holland; but combining my operations in such a manner, that it may be easy for me to get to the northward, in order to reach the tropic and arrive at the Isle of France by the end of November" (translated by L. A. Milet-Mureau). But the *Astrolabe* and the *Boussole* disappeared. Despite several search expeditions, including one under the guidance of Admiral Bruni d'Entrecasteaux in 1791 and one led by Dumont d'Urville around 1827, the 219 men of Lapérouse's expedition were never found. Around the same time, a British officer claimed that an American captain sailing in the South Sea had met the inhabitants of a group of islands surrounded by reefs and had seen in their hands a cross of the order of St. Louis, and medals like those worn by Lapérouse. But this story sounds a little too similar to another, older one, and there is no proof as to its truthfulness. In

1826, Peter Dillon, an Irish captain, was the first to discover evidence of two shipwrecked scows off the coast of Vanikoro, an islet east of the Solomon Islands.

It was not until 1964 that their wrecks were located. In 1999, Jean-Christophe Galipaud and divers of the Salomon Association surveyed ruins on Vanikoro, at the mouth of the Lawrence River. By excavating what looked like the foundations of a little fort occupied for several months and containing remains from the two ships, archeologists uncovered fragments of measuring instruments, a compass, gunflint, bullets, porcelain, nails, and bottles, proving that members of the expedition had survived. In 2003, researchers found the skeleton of a man of about thirty-two years of age. Was it that of chaplain Jean-André Mongez, of the astronomer Joseph Lepaute Dagelet, or the surgeon Jacques Joseph Le Cor? Now buried in Brest, he remains "the Unknown Man of Vanikoro." Two years later, south of Banie Island, what remained of the *Boussole* and the *Astrolabe* were formally identified. If one is to believe what the inhabitants of the archipelago have always said, then "the two ships ran aground during the night of a great storm. One sank, the other broke in two, and the survivors found refuge on the shore, at a place called Paiou." Five or six months later, some of them had managed to leave the island again on board a makeshift boat built with timber from the wrecks. Caught up in violent tribal wars, most of the Frenchmen remaining on the island had met a tragic fate, and the last living member of the expedition had passed away shortly before the arrival of Peter Dillon. In reality, no one really knows what happened to the Comte de Lapérouse and to those who took to the sea to leave Vanikoro.

In 1826, Peter Dillon, an Irish captain, was the first to discover evidence of two shipwrecked scows off the coast of Vanikoro.

IN THE SAME COLLECTION: